Officials' Signals

10

UNSPORTSMANLIKE CONDUCT
Arms outstretched,
palms down.

CONTINUING ACTION FOULS DISREGARDED
Move arms up and down.

11

SAFETY
Palms together over head.

12

LOSS OF DOWN
(Follows signal for foul.)
Tapping both shoulders
with fingertips.

13

PENALTY REFUSED, INCOMPLETE PASS, PLAY OVER, or **MISSED GOAL**
Sifting of hands in horizontal plane.

14

FIRST DOWN
Arm raised, then pointed toward
defensive team's goal.

15

DEAD BALL
or **NEUTRAL ZONE ESTABLISHED**
One arm aloft, open hand
(with fist closed—fourth down).

16

NO TIME-OUT or
TIME-IN WITH WHISTLE
Full arm circles to
simulate winding clock.

17

TIME-OUT
Hands crisscrossed
over head.
REFEREE'S TIME-OUT—
Same signal followed by
placing one hand on top of cap.
TOUCHBACK—same signal
followed by arm swung at side.

18

ILLEGAL PROCEDURE
or **TOUCHING**
Over and over rotation
of forearms in front of
body. Includes invalid
fair catch signal.

1971

Gloria —
Happy holiday...
Happy New Year.
Fondly,
Toni

How to Watch

Football

on Television

Foreword by Otto Graham

New York · The Viking Press

CHRIS SCHENKEL

HOW TO
WATCH FOOTBALL
ON TELEVISION

SECOND PRINTING SEPTEMBER 1964

First published in 1964 by The Viking Press, Inc.
625 Madison Avenue, New York, N.Y. 10022

Published simultaneously in Canada by
The Macmillan Company of Canada Limited

Library of Congress catalog card number: 64-20856
Printed in U.S.A. by Murray Printing Company

To the greatest six points in my life—

Fran, Tina, Ted, John, and Mother and Father
and
to the memory of Bert Bell

Foreword

It seemed only natural, having married a girl from Wabash, Indiana, and being from the neighboring state of Illinois myself, that I would link friendship with a guy born and raised in Bippus, Indiana. The fact that I went to college at Northwestern University and Chris Schenkel matriculated at rival Purdue made no difference. We were still within our neighboring states and, as neighbors are often apt to do, we became friends.

Our meeting took place so many years ago I can't remember the exact place or circumstances. I do recall, however, that after knowing Chris for just five minutes I got the feeling I had known him all my life. He has that folksy, down-to-earth quality that attracts respect. And respect is what all pro footballers have for Chris Schenkel.

In my ten years as a player with the Cleveland Browns (both in the All-America Conference and in the National Football League), I had little, if any, opportunity to hear Chris call the play-by-play of a pro game. But word used to get back to our locker room about the honesty and impartiality of his reporting, traits he obviously picked up as a student of the late Ted Husing. Players were also impressed by his knowledge of the game. As I became better acquainted with him, I found that Chris doesn't begin his broadcasts with the opening kickoff. He starts to study the week before—chatting with players and coaches on both sides; studying records and performance charts, statistics and medical reports. He's even apt to sit in on the screening of game films of the two teams involved in the upcoming clash. By the time he gets his air cue, this 145-pounder is a heavyweight of football knowledge. And it shows.

While I was quarterbacking the Browns, nothing was more pleasureful than beating the New York Giants. It was like putting whipped cream on top of a banana split. The most savory win of all, I think, was the first one in 1950, the Browns' inaugural year in the National Football League. The Giants knocked us off twice during the regular season, 16–0 and 17–13, but we both ended the year with identical records of 10–2, necessitating a playoff. The game was played in Cleveland (a decided advantage for us) on a frozen field in mid-December. I had thrown 14 touchdown passes that season, and the Giant defenses were prepared for an aerial barrage. So Coach Paul Brown pulled the unexpected and had me running quarterback sneaks all afternoon. With the help of brilliant fakes by Marion Motley and Dub Jones, along with an all-out team effort, we won the game, 8–3, and annexed the Eastern Conference Crown. The victory gave us enough buoyancy to take the championship game as well.

Today, nearly fifteen years later, I find myself a Giant

fan, although I never did play for the Mara Brothers. My job as Head Football Coach of the Coast Guard Academy team has me based in New London, Connecticut, which is within the area of the Giants' television broadcasts. This allows me to watch their games and hear Chris Schenkel's commentary during the entire season. I have come to learn at first hand why he is considered the dean of football reporters.

When the publishers invited me to write a foreword for this book, I considered it a pleasure. If I may be permitted to come out of player-retirement just long enough to throw one more pass, let me throw this at you: *How to Watch Football on Television* is very informative and interesting reading for fans and non-fans alike. I know you'll enjoy it and find it helpful as reference material as you watch your favorite team play. And who knows, maybe I'll find an idea or two within its pages to teach my College All-Stars in our annual game against the NFL champions in Chicago. But then, they'll probably be reading the book too.

Commander Otto Graham

Head Football Coach
U. S. Coast Guard Academy
New London, Connecticut

Contents

Diagrams

Acknowledgments

Many people have been helpful to me in the writing of this book, and I am grateful to all of them. I would particularly like to thank Pete Rozelle, Commissioner of the National Football League; Jim Kensil, Director of Public Relations for the National Football League, and his staff; Rose Marie O'Reilly and her staff in the CBS-TV Research Department; William MacPhail, Vice President of CBS-TV sports, and his staff; Pat Summerall, my colleague on telecasts of the Giants' games; Tom Brookshier, former defensive halfback of the Philadelphia Eagles and now a sports announcer with WCAU in Philadelphia; and John Chanin, Producer of CBS Radio's "Worldwide Sports."

1. The Evolution of Today's Football

New York Giant rookie halfback Charlie Killett threw open the door to the Taj Mahal of dressing rooms beneath the first-base stands of Yankee Stadium. What he saw was an area about four times the size of what he had been used to at Central High in Helena, Arkansas, or at Memphis State University. The floor was carpeted from wall to wall, and each player was assigned to a walk-in stall with enough room not only for clothes and equipment, but for all the razor blades, shaving cream, and non-greasy adult stuff he'd care to endorse. It was October 8, 1963, and the Giants had already played four football games, but all on the road. This was their first opportunity to move into the comfortable surroundings of Yankee Stadium. The Yankees themselves had occupied the place throughout the World Series.

Killett held the door open for head coach Allie Sherman, who was close behind. "I'm sorry, kid," said Sherman, "but this is the best we can do until the Yankees clear out of the regular dressing room."

"This is good enough for me." Killett smiled. "Good" was to say the least. This dressing room is symbolic of champions and the growth of professional football.

I'm sure that when the first group of admitted professionals played their inaugural game in 1895, receiving ten bucks apiece for the efforts, none of them ever imagined that one day players would dress for a game in a locker room with wall-to-wall carpeting. Latrobe, Pennsylvania, a small town near Pittsburgh, which later would receive much publicity as the home town of golf's fabulous Arnold Palmer, fielded the first team of pros, who were sponsored by the local YMCA. They won that first game, defeating Jeannette, a team from another Pittsburgh suburb, 12–0, and for the next decade Latrobe was one of the big powerhouses in pro ball, attracting a number of the top college stars of the day, many of whom gave up eligible years to play for pay.

The fad caught on, and soon teams began to spring up throughout Pennsylvania and in upstate New York. Rhode Island, New Jersey, and Ohio then got into the act, but the whole thing was still run in a very unbusinesslike atmosphere. The players were now getting a little more than ten dollars a game, with a few of the big name ex-college stars receiving as much as five hundred dollars. But contracts didn't exist, and it was very common to see a standout player competing for one team one week and another team the following week. Knute Rockne, who in later years was to make Pat O'Brien a household word, faced the Columbus Panhandles six times in 1915, each time with a different club.

This type of confusion reigned in professional football for its first fifteen or twenty years, and while spectator interest was high, attendance figures were low. It would take calm, intelligent minds to establish a working, profitable organization which would also appeal to the fans. Perhaps a speech by a college coach became the goading, as well as the guiding, force. Bob Zuppke, the head football coach at the University of Illinois, was a speaker at a banquet for his 1918 graduating team. "Why is it," asked Zuppke, "that just when you players are beginning to know something about football after three years, you stop playing? Football ends a man's career just when it should be beginning."

A mild increase in professional football interest began shortly after World War I, and such names as George Halas, Jim Thorpe, and Red Grange began to make their impression on the American public. This was not the specialized type of football we know today, with separate teams for offense and defense, and distinctive units for punts, kickoffs, and the like. This was the kind of football where the top men, the starters, played both ways—offense and defense—and it got pretty bloody. Equipment was not standardized or legalized (perhaps we should say illegalized); in fact, Thorpe used a shoulder pad not only made of leather and padding, but also covered with sheet metal. Not that Thorpe needed such a weapon for his offensive mastery. It was just that, if he hadn't come up with this form of protection, an opponent might have used something equally lethal against him.

Thorpe played for the Canton Bulldogs from 1915 to 1925, and his gridiron performances during that period were a strong impetus for a wise group of businessmen who met and fertilized the egg that was to hatch into the

National Football League. An automobile showroom for the Ralph E. Hay Company of Canton, Ohio, served as the assembly hall for this group in September 1920, and eleven delegates were on hand to write a charter. Thorpe was there, representing Canton. So was George Halas, on the payroll of a starch company in Decatur, Illinois. Team agents from Cleveland, Dayton, Akron, Massillon, Rochester (New York), Rock Island (Illinois), Muncie (Indiana), Hammond (Indiana), and Chicago were also there. The union was given a name—the American Professional Football Association. Thorpe was elected president; Stan Cofall (Massillon), vice-president; A. F. Ranney (Akron), secretary-treasurer; and a franchise went for all of a hundred dollars. These eleven men loved football, and they seemed to be astute businessmen, but for some reason they couldn't couple the two and make it work. The schedules were so confusing, when any schedules existed at all, that three teams announced themselves champions, and one (Massillon) threw in the towel.

The following spring a Columbus sportswriter named Joe Carr, who doubled as manager of the Columbus Panhandles, reorganized the association with a new slate of officers. Carr himself was elected president, and his next eighteen years of leadership were to give professional football a foundation from which it would never topple. While schedules were still on a week-to-week operation— the undertaking was suffering from growing pains— franchises were being shifted to more profitable areas, and Carr and his associates were constantly busy with their paper work. Green Bay, Wisconsin, got itself a football team in August of 1921 (a later dispute over the alleged use of ineligible players caused the franchise to be returned to the league, but it was reawarded to Curly Lambeau, the former Notre Dame backfield great, in June of 1922). George Halas's Decatur franchise was moved to Chicago and renamed the Bears. The organization's name was changed from the American Professional Football Association to the National Football League, and the group was on its way. But even with that early, mild success, none of the club owners ever visualized their teams playing before 80,000 fans in one stadium at one time, and certainly none of them, not even the believers in Buck Rogers, could see a thing called television, which one day would permit a game to be seen in more than 13 million American homes in one afternoon.

The league began to mushroom. Philadelphia, then New York, and then Detroit were awarded franchises, and the league office began to resemble a true business organization. Carr wrote the first constitution and by-laws in 1926, and they included a clause inspired by the football feats of one Harold "Red" Grange while he was a student at the University of Illinois. That clause prevented any member team of the National Football League from inducing or attempting to induce any college player to engage in professional football until his class at college had graduated. Violation brought a fine of $1000, or the loss of the franchise, or both. Professional football had now publicized its integrity, while at the same time it kept its free-of-charge farm system alive.

Franchises moved from city to city; some dropped out, others came in. Player limits were raised, extra officials were hired, and the treasuries grew. But a solid link was still somehow missing, and in 1932 the link appeared. A Boston franchise was awarded to George Preston Marshall, a vigorous man with a flair for show business as well as for business. Marshall put an end to the years of turmoil by first establishing a uniform schedule where every team played the same number of games. Working together with such men as George Halas (Chicago Bears), Art Rooney (Pittsburgh Steelers), and Tim Mara (New York Giants), Marshall divided the league into two divisions (or conferences), east and west; established a standard set of playing rules; and suggested the championship play-off game. With his love of show business, and assisted by his one-time movie star wife (Corinne Griffith), he started the Washington Redskin band and the magnificent half-time shows.

Now the National Football League was a machine. It got some additional oiling from the late Bert Bell while Bell was on the board of directors of the Philadelphia Eagles. He proposed the college-player draft to give equal balance to each team in the league. The club finishing last would get the first pick of available college talent; the one finishing next to last would pick next; and so on up the line. This system kept the so-called prestige teams from attracting the best players and building dynasties that could only destroy the league. By the mid-thirties, and certainly by the outbreak of World War II, the system was proving its worth.

In 1940 the use of a new weapon, rarely seen before, was to be unveiled in the championship game. This weapon was to revolutionize football and give it still another surge of popularity. It was, of course, the T-formation. George Halas had been experimenting with variations of the T, exploring all its faking possibilities and its effectiveness in the employment of the forward pass. After studying films of the Washington Redskins (winners of the Eastern Conference), Halas, whose Bears would oppose the Skins in the championship game, built a series of plays which he thought would work against Washington.

There was a full house at Griffith Stadium as Washington kicked off to the Bears. It was a confident Washington team. During the regular season they had downed Chicago, 7–3. But Halas, the man who had seen to it that the forward pass was legal from anywhere behind the line of scrimmage, and who was instrumental in moving the goal posts to the goal line, was equally confident in his T-formation. On first and ten, George McAfee took a handoff and went wide to his right for an 8-yard gain. On second down, quarterback Sid Luckman faked to his halfback, who plowed into the line, taking the Washington defenders with him. Luckman then handed off to Bill Osmanski, his fullback, who had faked a block to the opposite side. Osmanski skirted wide for a 68-yard touchdown romp and, as they say in football, he's still running. That play was the backbreaker. Chicago went on to win the game by an overwhelming 73-0, with ten different Bears scoring eleven touchdowns.

Now the game had really arrived, but it could be enjoyed only by the fans who lived in or near the cities with franchises. Radio brought the action to the other areas of the country, but with radio the public had to visualize what was happening. They couldn't really see for themselves how much more advanced this game was than what they were used to seeing on the high-school or college fields. Fewer than a half-million people witnessed NFL games during the 1933 season.

By 1940, attendance for an eleven-game schedule went over the million mark. A dozen-game schedule was played in 1948, but attendance figures were not appreciably higher. That was the year, though, that professional football and television began to grow together. In 1948 the Bears televised six home games for $4800. In 1951 Chicago had an eleven-city network, but the Bears actually had to pay two of the stations (in St. Louis and Louisville) to carry the games, and they suffered a deficit of $1750 on the television project. Attendance in that year was approaching the 2-million mark.

The television industry recognized a good thing and rolled up its sleeves. Tom McMahon of the Dumont Television Network arranged for the purchase of the exclusive rights to televise, broadcast, and film the world-championship football games of the National Football League for 1951, 1952, 1953, 1954, and 1955 for $475,000. Compare this to the record $1,800,000 per game CBS paid for the radio and television rights to the 1964 and 1965 championships, and realize that only nine years have passed since the rights went for less than $100,000. That will give you an idea of the tremendous growth professional football and television have enjoyed.

Television coverage was increasing, the ratings were growing higher, and so was the attendance at the ball parks. Dumont televised five regular-season games in 1951, which produced an average audience Nielsen rating of 7.4 and an average audience share of 17.9 per cent NFL attendance for 1951 was 1,913,019. By 1954 Dumont was televising twelve regular-season games, producing an average audience rating of 11.2 and an average audience share of 36.9 per cent. Attendance soared to 2,190,571.

These figures reflect only the games televised on Sundays. Professional football was no longer the property of just the franchised cities. Television was bringing it into Bippus, Indiana, and Charlotte, North Carolina; Portland, Oregon, and Bangor, Maine. The great heroes that fans had only read about, they could now see in the comfort of their own homes. Everyone had a fifty-yard-line seat in his living room.

The growth continued. In 1962 the fourteen teams in the National Football League became richer by $9,300,000 when they entered into an agreement with the Columbia Broadcasting System for exclusive television coverage of the fourteen-week regular-season schedule in 1962 and 1963. The contract followed the passage of a federal law in 1961 which exempted professional football, basketball, baseball, and hockey leagues from the antitrust law in the area of a single network television contract. The new agreement between the NFL and CBS provided for equal distribution of the television-rights money among the member clubs of the NFL. William C. MacPhail, Vice-President of CBS Television Sports, remarked that the nationwide interest in NFL games and the support by television fans made the contract possible. "National League Football," added MacPhail, "is the outstanding sports series on network television, and CBS is anticipating eagerly the televising of these games. The telecasts are vital and popular community events."

So true! In 1962 the average TV audience for Sunday telecasts rose to 14.2, while the average audience share catapulted to 46.8 per cent. The 1962 season attendance for fourteen teams was 4,003,421. It went still higher in 1963: average audience rating, 16.5; average audience share, 50.6 per cent; fourteen-team attendance, 4,163,643. On January 24, 1964, a joint NFL–CBS news release had the impact of an atom bomb. That day representatives of the three major networks had gathered in the office of Pete Rozelle, commissioner of the NFL, to bid for the rights to the 1964–65 regular-season games. Based on the prior years' progression, the good guess among members of the press was 15 million dollars for the two years. As Rozelle read the first quotation (NBC), it was obvious how wrong everybody was. ABC's bid was next to be read, and it was well above the NBC quotation. The last bid to be opened was the one from CBS, and it turned out to be the winner—but barely the winner—$28,200,000 for two years. It meant that each club in the league would be the recipient of a million dollars for each of two years. It spelled automatic profit for the owners, and for Rozelle that day it meant a feeling of great pride.

Two weeks later, NBC announced it had made a deal with the rival American Football League for a five-year period, which would guarantee each member club nearly a million dollars for each of the five years. If the AFL was in danger of sinking, it had just been thrown a life-preserver. The strength of network television had come to the rescue.

CBS did not stop with its rich package. It also acquired the rights to the 1964 and 1965 league championship games for $1,800,000 per game, double the $926,000 fee paid for the 1963 title game by NBC. It was the highest price ever paid by a network to obtain a one-day sports event. And there was no bidding. Commissioner Rozelle explained that negotiations for the two-year agreement were limited to CBS-TV because each of the other two major networks had contracts with the American Football League to televise regular-season games during the period of the contract, and one of those networks was committed to carry the AFL play-off game in 1964. Therefore it was considered in the best interest of the National Football League to keep its championship game free of any possible conflict of interest, especially in the area of promotion.

NBC and ABC were dismayed and expressed surprise that there was no bidding. An NBC spokesman said that they were planning to bid at least 2 million dollars for the rights, and 3 million dollars if all three networks participated in the bidding. The friction is understandable. The championship game in 1963 reached 70 per cent of the American viewers who own television sets—a handsome figure to throw at a potential sponsor looking for saturation with his product.

It has been said that baseball is the national pastime, but on television, it's all football. In 1964 the professional football teams will receive nearly 22 million dollars from television, not counting the revenues from championship, all-star, and runner-up games. This figure exceeds baseball income from television by almost 6 million dollars.

Unique in 1964 will be weekday night telecasts of NFL games, and several doubleheaders on Sunday. Viewers will be able to watch a complete game in the East, followed by a complete game in the West—nearly six hours of professional football in one afternoon.

This has prompted some people to be concerned over the possibility of oversaturation. Johnny Unitas, the great quarterback of the Baltimore Colts, feels that overexposure could kill football. Said Unitas, "People are going to get tired of seeing so much pro football on television. Part of the lure has been the fact that it hasn't been easily attainable for the fans." Maybe so. But the public right now is demanding it. Those living in blacked-out areas have a void in their lives when they can't see a ball game. People in the New York area will pack a picnic lunch, load up a carful of fans, and drive seventy-five miles to Connecticut motels which lie outside of the blackout screen, in order to see their Giants play. Some of the motels sell season tickets ($80 for seven home games), which give you the right to use the room and the TV set just for the duration of the game. During the half-time intermission, one or two of the motels provide entertainment—marching bands, cheerleaders, and all the other color usually found between the second and third quarters. This type of enthusiasm, it seems to me, will take a long time to reach the oversaturation point. I think fans will be glued to television sets watching professional football as long as there's professional football to watch. And that will make me, my wife, and all my heirs very happy.

My entrance into any of the stadiums during the NFL season remains a moving experience, even after twelve years. In fact, the excitement of seeing capacity crowds has increased, rather than diminished; so much so that when the final gun sounds on a Sunday afternoon, I can hardly wait for the next Sunday to come around. It's like having fourteen wedding days in a row. And, judging from the increasing enthusiasm generated by the ever-growing number of fans, that feeling must be contagious. I can recommend no better way of enjoying football than to head for a stadium where a National Football League game is scheduled.

Lately, however, this has become a problem. Some clubs are completely sold out six months prior to the start of the season, making it impossible for thousands and thousands of their followers to purchase tickets. The next best thing, then, is to watch football on television. True, the tube may not engulf you in the wave of excitement found inside the stadium, but it comes close, and, of course, it has other distinct advantages. The close-up lens of the camera almost makes you part of every play. You're always on the fifty-yard line. There's no weather problem inside your own home—no having to sit exposed to rain, or snow or subfreezing temperatures. And the lady of the house can make your favorite snack or beverage a lot more attractive than the stadium vender does.

There is no necessity to turn to the person sitting next to you and engage in a guessing game as to what exactly took place on the field. The TV announcers, long on experience (some have even played the game), are quick to explain the play in the best way they know how. But the announcers still receive hundreds of letters a week from inquisitive viewers anxious to know still more about a specific play or player, or a new formation, or a strategic move.

I have tried in this book, to the best of my ability, to incorporate concise answers to the questions most frequently asked by viewers. There are condensed descriptions of every position on the team, of basic offensive and defensive formations, of key plays; and all the other information which I believe will aid you in getting more enjoyment and knowledge from watching football on television.

Players' numbers have become pretty consistent with the positions they play. In watching the game on your screen, familiarity with these numbers (as shown in the accompanying table) will assist you. Numbers of defen-

---

PLAYERS' NUMBERS

0–49 Offensive or defensive backs

50–59 Centers

60–69 Guards

70–79 Tackles

80–89 Ends

sive linemen usually follow the same pattern, while those of the linebackers will generally fall within the fifty-to-eighty-nine bracket. There are, of course, exceptions. Occasionally a player comes along who has achieved particularly high status on the college gridiron. So well known is he, not just by name but by number, that he is allowed to keep that same number while a pro, even if it doesn't coincide with the accepted practice just described. Other players may have a lucky number which they insist on wearing. Rather than upset the player by assigning another number, it's often psychologically wiser for the team to assign the lucky number and trust that the player's horoscope works out.

As football has grown, it has developed a language all its own. To the uninitiated these terms can be a total mystery; to the rabid fan they are as familiar as his own name. Where it has seemed necessary to explain a particular term I have done so in the text. If you are still puzzled, however, I have included a glossary at the end of this book of the most frequently used "lingo."

I have taken most of my examples in this book from the teams comprising the National Football League, not necessarily because I am partial to this league above all others, but because I have spent every Sunday during twelve football seasons broadcasting NFL games. I feel myself fortunate to include many players, owners, coaches, and officials in the league among my close friends. All of them made these chapters possible.

2. Offense

In his book on football, Giants' head coach Allie Sherman calls the game "War." "The coach is the general; the quarterback, the commanding officer; the players, the soldiers." A further description, in the case of the pros, is that football is big business. For the owners and shareholders, it's another money-making venture. For the coaches and players, it's their way of earning a living. The pro doesn't subject his body to a severe pummeling week after week, from July through December, in response to the enthusiasm of a dozen curvy cheerleaders and for the glory of the old university. That's gone when the diploma finds its way to the top shelf of an attic closet. The pro gives the lumps and absorbs the bruises for his own individual paycheck. He fights for his team to win, but he has the necessary resources to promote his own cause as well. The Mercury Division of the Ford Motor Company wishes nothing but the best for its parental father—but don't think the young upstart wouldn't love to outsell the old man once in a while.

The professional football player's desire to win is largely economic. If his team finishes first, it enters into a championship game, and he receives more money. The bigger the role he plays in his team's achievement, the better his position at the bargaining table the following year. The team's method of winning is basic—score more points than the other team. Its mechanics are the same as those used by the high schools and colleges, though more highly polished.

THE BASIC FORMATIONS

There are two distinct formations used in football—the "T" and the single wing, with the latter being almost totally out of use today. Variations of both formations are used by the versatile coach who is quick to adapt to the specific talents of his personnel.

The Tight "T"

The viewer is quick to recognize the "T" formation because of its frequency of use. In the "tight" variation, the line is balanced; that is, an equal number of men are on either side of the center, with tackle to tackle lined up foot to foot, and the ends split one to two yards from their tackles. The quarterback is positioned directly behind his center; the fullback completes that straight line, about three to four yards behind the quarterback. The halfbacks are generally in line with, or slightly to the inside of, their tackles, and flank the fullback; the center and the four backs thus forming the letter "T."

The Split "T"

In the "split" variation, the development of which is credited to Don Faurot while he was head coach at the University of Missouri, there are gaps of different lengths between the linemen. This formation is designed to spread the defense and give the men up front a better blocking angle. Each coach, again, will space his men according to how they perform best.

"T" Variations

There are dozens, perhaps hundreds, of ways a coach can shift his offensive attack: men in motion, flankers, tight ends, winged "T," double-wing, shotgun, "A." The hour-after-hour screening of an opposing team's defense might light the idea bulb. A visit to a gypsy tea room or a bad dream might produce even more thoughts. Once the blueprint of the foundation is dry, then comes the building of the plays—running, passing, and kicking.

The tight "T" formation

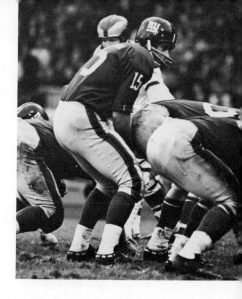

THE
QUARTERBACK

The major catalyst in the offensive attack is, of course, the quarterback. He's the hardest player to find and the most difficult to develop, and he commands the highest salary on the club. He's the chairman of the board of that business out on the field. And the reasons are obvious.

A quarterback's qualifications are as demanding as the Boy Scout's oath. He must have trip-hammer reflexes; he must have speed and agility. His sleight-of-hand must rival the secret operations of a magician. Brains, a clear mind, coolness under fire, the ability to command and to make the right decision at the right time—these are all part of a quarterback's basic requirements. And, perhaps most important, he must be able to throw that football. The forward pass has become the nuclear warhead in the pro's offense. During the regular 1963 season in the National Football League, the 14 teams scored a total of 492 touchdowns; 302 were via the air route. That's an average of more than 61 per cent. No longer is third down the pass-play down. A team with a needle-threading passer, good receivers, and a strong forward wall is just as apt to throw on first down from behind its own goal line as it is on second or third down in relatively safe territory.

The football player's bible, the play book, grows thicker each year, and the section on pass patterns is the heartiest mushroom. Therefore, the quarterback's statistics grow from season to season. In 1961, Cleveland's Milt Plum was the passing champion for the second consecutive years, because of his 58.6 per cent completion average. He also had a low of 3.3 per cent interceptions. In that same year Sonny Jurgensen of the Philadelphia Eagles led the league in completions (235), yards gained passing (3723), and touchdown passes (32).

In 1962 Bart Starr of the Green Bay Packers grabbed the individual championship with a 62.5 per cent completion average, and lowered the interception percentage to 3.2. Green Bay, however, is known for its ground attack, and Starr completed only 12 touchdown passes. The honor for most touchdown passes in that year went to the bald-headed fellow, Y. A. Tittle of the New York Giants. He tossed a record-breaking 33, with the book entry coming in the final minute of the final game of the season. The Giants led Dallas by four points, 35–31, and had a first down on the Cowboys' eight. The armchair quarterbacks called for four clock-moving running plays. Don't give Dallas a chance to get the ball. Stall till the final gun. But the Giants wanted more than the Eastern crown, and more for the quarterback who led them to that goal than just a back-pat—they wanted Tittle's name in the record book. In the privacy of the huddle they urged him to pass for a score. And pass he did, into the waiting arms of Joe Walton for number 33. In the same season Tittle threw 7 scores in one game (against the Redskins on October 28), tying the record for most touchdown passes in one game, a record shared by Adrian Burk and Sid Luckman.

In 1963, at an age when most football players think about an extra sweater on chilly days and a heating pad when the air is damp, Tittle was back in uniform, acting fifteen years younger and rewriting the record books. He won the individual passing championship for the first time in his fourteen years in the league, and led in three of the four categories used to rank a passer. He passed for a record 36 touchdowns, had a 60.2 per cent completion average, and averaged 8.57 yards per throw. Further to demonstrate how deadly Tittle was with his passes last year, Johnny Unitas of Baltimore ranked second in completions but connected for only 20 touchdowns. And the Cardinals' Charley Johnson tossed 28 touchdown passes but was rated fifth over-all in the league.

The year 1963 also saw a twenty-four-year old record dusted off and shoved aside to welcome a new addition. George Izo of the Washington Redskins brought a partisan opening-day crowd of Cleveland Browns fans to various degrees of pain and excitement when he threw a 99-yard touchdown aerial to the swift Bobby Mitchell. The toss tied the record set in 1939, also by a Redskin quarterback, Frankie Filchock, to Andy Farkas, in a game against the Pittsburgh Steelers. Cleveland fans left Municipal Stadium in a happy frame of mind—the Browns had dumped Washington, 37–14—but as they filed onto the Lake Erie easements, they were still talking about that long one from Izo to Mitchell.

So the quarterback is more than bread and butter or meat and potatoes. He's a seven-course meal, all rolled into one, and in later paragraphs we'll attempt to make you his counterpart in the comfort of your own living room.

A T-formation quarterback can throw a forward pass to five eligible receivers—his two ends and the three other backs. This quintet works many hours in practice sessions with the passer, until each pass pattern forms an imaginary groove in the turf. The precision and timing must be exact. At times the receiver's hands or parts of his body become the passer's target. On other occasions, the receiver must head for a spot on the field, and if the calculations are correct the ball reaches that spot at the same time he does. The receiver thus becomes a most important factor in a quarterback's success. The working relationship between a quarterback and his receivers rivals the best love affair.

THE ENDS

Ends in the National Football League, with one or two exceptions, are tall; their height makes them easier to spot going downfield and helps them outreach a defender trying to intercept. They must possess speed, and those who aren't quite so tall need still more speed. An end must also possess big hands, with fingers able to grasp the football with the same deftness as a surgeon's in grasping a scalpel. He must also know his quarterback. Does he throw a bullet-type pass, or a soft, looping pass? Does the ball usually head upward, or point downward; or does it move in a straight line? He must also have the ability to outmaneuver the opposition, or, as I once described a Del Shofner move, "to fake 'em right out of their jocks." (This comment brought me a lot of amusing mail.)

I remember one beautiful series of fakes in a Browns–Giants game during the 1962 season. Rich Kreitling, Cleveland's 6-foot-2 offensive end, was split wide to the left. Ray Renfro was a flanker right. Quarterback Jim Ninowski took the snap from center and quickly pitched out to his fullback, Jimmy Brown, who started a wide sweep. Renfro moved ahead as if to form a blocking pattern for Brown. But he suddenly stopped, reversed his field, and took a handoff from Brown while heading for the opposite side. Renfro then handed the ball back to Ninowski, who rifled a long clothesliner to Kreitling, who had drifted down and across into the end zone while the triple reverse was in progress. The Giants' defense was numbed and embarrassed.

New York, with Tittle, is a passing team. Y. A. will pass on any down, and in any position on the field. He has the confidence it takes to be a pro quarterback, not only in his own passing ability, but in his receivers as well. And in recent years the Giants have had great receivers —Del Shofner, Kyle Rote, Frank Gifford, and Bob Schnelker, just to mention four.

The Tight End

The tight end (the one positioned about a yard from his tackle) has the additional responsibility of blocking a defensive end or corner linebacker, and sometimes a defensive halfback. So in addition to having glue-fingers for pass-catching, the tight end is big, strong, and fast. One of the best in the National Football League is Green Bay's Ron Kramer. This former Michigan All-American, whose brain contains an encyclopedia of football techniques, is 6 foot 3 and weighs in at 240. I've seen him slaughter a defensive end or tackle and, in the same motion, knock off a linebacker as well. One play later, I've seen him ease under a Bart Starr pass, run over a defensive back, and outfake a safety man to go into pay dirt standing up. When a Ron Kramer type shows up at training camp for the first time, he creates the same type of salivary action in a coach's mouth as the thought of a dill pickle creates in mine. And that's good!

THE FULLBACK

When America's space scientists began envisioning orbital flights, they had to come up with a power plant capable of tremendous speed and thrust to get that payload into free flight. Maybe they were thinking of the fullback in football when the right idea hit. This is the human power plant who absorbs more punishment than any other offensive back. He's a ball carrier who can be called upon to run either inside or outside. He's a pass receiver. And when he's not carrying the ball or faking a carry, or running out as a pass receiver, he's leading interference for the halfback. This is the guy who must get you that yard for the first down or the touchdown, when about 2500 pounds of bull-meat is intent on not letting it happen. This is the same guy who must become a sprinter when he breaks into the open. And he's the same guy who becomes his quarterback's bodyguard as the pass patterns unfold.

The Giants' Alex Webster, who I think is one of the most underrated fullbacks in the league, was sidelined by a bad back for most of the 1963 season, but he finished ninth in rushing in 1962, and in 1961 he was third, having carried the ball 196 times for 928 yards and a 4.7 average per carry—most impressive, when you consider the Giants are primarily a passing team. In my estimation, too, "Big Red," as he's known around the league, has no peer when it comes to blocking.

Green Bay's Jimmy Taylor is another all-time great fullback. If he lacks anything, it's tremendous speed. But Taylor's initial acceleration is like the launching of a rocket. His thrusts through the line are violent, his legs like ramrods as he plows through to daylight. Taylor's name had asterisks beside it in the 1962 record book; his 272 carries and 1474 yards gained were high for the year. And his 19 touchdowns set a record for one season, previously held by Steve Van Buren (with the Eagles in 1945) and Jimmy Brown (with the Browns in 1958). And while we're on the subject of Jimmy Brown, there will never be another book written on professional football that won't contain his name. In fact, a good project for any English major in college aspiring to a master's degree would be to write a term paper containing a thousand new adjectives describing Jimmy Brown. All the old ones have been used up.

Oldtimers will talk until they're blue in the face about Red Grange, Bronko Nagurski, and Jim Thorpe—and those names stir my emotions too—but Jimmy Brown is the greatest running back I have ever seen. To me, he's the .400 hitter, the anchor man on a relay team, and the heavyweight champion of the world, all rolled up into one.

When he came to Cleveland in 1957, following his graduation from Syracuse University, Brown immediately proceeded to lead the NFL in rushing. He dominated that category for four more years, his streak snapped by Green Bay's Jimmy Taylor in 1962. But, he was back on top in 1963 for the sixth time in his seven years as a pro, gaining a record 1863 yards in 291 attempts for a 6.4-yards-per-carry average. His longest run of the year was an 80-yard sprint against the Redskins on September 15, good for six points, but I'll never forget him on the fifth Sunday of the 1963 season when he blew a key game against the Giants wide open with his whole bag of tricks. The Giants were opening their home season, following a four-game road trip which saw them win three and drop one. They were seeking their third consecutive Eastern title. Cleveland had rolled over Washington, Dallas, Los Angeles, and Pittsburgh and was the talk of the Eastern Conference, if not of the entire league. Brown scored his first of three touchdowns by leaping high over the top of an immovable Giant goal-line defense. He produced the second after grabbing a screen pass from Quarterback Frank Ryan and faking three Giants on his 72-yard jaunt. And to prove his amazing versatility and intelligence, he scored the third time on a 32-yard option play which he set up by cheating a couple of steps to the inside of his normal backfield position. This gave him a jump on Sam Huff, New York's middle linebacker, and allowed him to get outside. Once clear of the line of scrimmage, he cut back sharply, reversing his field, and as he headed for the touchdown all by himself, he was grinning from ear to ear. Watch Jimmy Brown very carefully the next time he appears on your television screen. You will marvel at the way he dips his shoulder, or the way he drives his legs into a linebacker, or the way he veers from one direction to another. Notice, too, how he assaults the high tacklers by driving his free arm upward in an effort to break the grip. This is Jimmy Brown, a human marvel, and one of the all-time great football players.

THE HALFBACKS

The pros have two offensive halfbacks in the lineup, although it has become commonplace for one of them to be positioned outside the tight end, instead of alongside his fullback. Therefore, he has been dubbed the flanker-back, and is more responsible for catching passes than for running. Both the halfback and the flanker-back must possess a lot of speed and, in the case of the running halfback, must be big and strong enough to elude, or knock over, a defensive back. Since both are eligible pass receivers, they must have the qualifications of an end, as well as the requisites for a running back. If both halfbacks are equally good at catching passes and at running with the ball, a coach may vary his offense and flank both at the same time; or flank one and send the other in motion to put them both into a pass pattern. And since one of the fundamentals of football is to force the defense to react in one direction and then strike in the other, the halfback will often act as a decoy into the line to set up another type of play. The halfback, then, must be able to absorb the

punishment dished out by those 270-pound tackles and those 240-pound linebackers.

The Running Halfback

One of the more impressive running halfbacks last season was Tommy Mason of the Minnesota Vikings. He has good speed, good fakes, and good hands. The former Tulane star, in his third year as a pro, gained 763 yards rushing, scored 7 touchdowns on the ground and 2 on passes, and averaged 4.6 yards per carry.

In my twelve years of covering professional football on television, though, no halfback in the National Football League has surpassed the performances of Green Bay's Paul Hornung. This may create some furor around Philadelphia, where the name of Steve Van Buren is still engraved in the minds of Eagle fans. Steve was winding up his illustrious career when pro football on television was being nurtured, but I must honestly add that, as a spectator of football long before I began broadcasting the game on TV, Van Buren gave me many thrills to remember, the most vivid being his 5-yard plow through the snow to give the Eagles a 7–0 championship win over the Chicago Cardinals in 1948.

Getting back to Hornung, though, I have to call him the last of the triple-threat men in pro ball today. We have become so used to seeing specialists who are good in just one particular phase of the game that our eyes blink when a Hornung comes along. Paul can run, pass, and kick, and if you take a poll of defensive players around the league, they'll tell you he's a hell of a blocker as well. But you can see all this for yourself whenever he's on your screen.

Hornung came to the Packers from Notre Dame (apparently he's partial to green) in 1957 as their number-one bonus draft choice. He was a two-time All-American while with the Fighting Irish and collected the Heisman Trophy (awarded to the outstanding college athlete), to boot. Paul wasted no time, once in the Green Bay uniform, proving the college honors were no figment of a press agent's imagination. From 1957 through 1962 he moved to second place among the all-time Packer scorers, second only to the remarkable Don Hutson. During this period, he hit pay dirt 44 times and kicked 54 field goals and 149 extra points, for a total of 575 points. In these six seasons he amassed a total of 2798 yards rushing, and in 1960 he led the league in the most points scored in one season, 176. That same year and the year after he was elected to the all-pro team. In 1962, despite a series of knee injuries, Hornung scored 7 touchdowns, kicked 14 extra points and 6 field goals, and completed 4 out of 6 passes. And while the 1961 37–0 championship game victory over the Giants was certainly a Green Bay team effort, there's no doubt that the first key break in the game came on Hornung's snare of a Bart Starr pass and his beautiful faking of the Giant defenders for a 26-yard gain. The remainder of the afternoon saw him score 19 points, one more than half of the Packers' total.

When Paul Hornung is not running or passing, you'll see him chopping down the opposition like a 275-pound tackle. When he's passing, he'll almost always make the completion, and when he's running, there's bound to be yardage gained. And when he's running with the goal line in clear sight, the Packer score is sure to advance by six points. And if he can't bring it in *under* the goal posts, he'll kick it *over* the goalposts. Paul Hornung—one of the finest competitors in professional football today.

The Flanker Back

As far as flankers go, Bobby Joe Conrad of the St. Louis Cardinals and Bobby Mitchell of the Washington Redskins dominated the league in 1963. Conrad caught 73 passes, 10 of them for touchdowns; Mitchell snagged 69, 7 of them good for scores. The fleet-footed Redskin also had the best one-game performance last year, although in a losing cause. In Washington's losing effort to Pittsburgh on November 17, Mitchell caught 11 passes for 218 yards and 2 touchdowns. Bobby's performances become even more impressive when you consider that the Redskins won only three games last year, and finished next to last in the Eastern Conference.

I'm a little partial to a couple of New Yorkers, though, as far as flankers and ends go. Frank Gifford gets the nod as the gutsiest, and Kyle Rote as one of the greatest. Gifford was racked up badly in a game with the Eagles

in November of 1960; his brain concussion was so severe
it kept him away from pro ball during the entire 1961
season. But Giff's a stout competitor. He became one
of the few professionals to make a comeback, and what
made it even tougher was leaving his familiar halfback spot to become a flanker. Rote worked with Gifford,
taught him all the crafty moves to deceive the defense
and make up for the waning speed. Gifford caught 39
passes good for 796 yards and 7 big touchdowns in 1962,
and last season he hauled in 42 for 657 yards and, again,
7 touchdowns.

After some twenty years of competitive football, Gifford's mind and reactions are still razor-sharp. In the
crucial game against Pittsburgh last December at Yankee
Stadium, Frank went in motion to his left from the right
flanker position and grabbed a pitchout from Y. A. Tittle.
He raced for the outside on the halfback-option play, but
found his path blocked by 270-pound John Baker. He
faked a pass downfield, quickly reversed his field, and
started back for the right side. Trapped again by Pittsburgh defenders, Gifford lateraled to Greg Larsen, the
Giant center, who is not used to handling the ball in an
upright position. Larsen quickly released the "apple" to
Tittle, who broke into a smile as he flipped it back to Gifford. Frank again went to his right and threw a forward
pass intended for Aaron Thomas, who all this time was
maneuvering in the end zone in much the same way a
basketball player moves in and out of the keyhole. The
pass was batted down by Steeler defensive halfback Glenn
Glass. Said Gifford in the dressing room after the game,
"If I tossed the ball back to Tittle after he gave it to me
the second time, he would have broken up right then and
there."

Before Kyle Rote retired as a player to become offensive backfield coach, he was a threat as a runner, passer, and pass-receiver. An injury to his knee curtailed his running ability, so he was shifted to the outside and became one of the most skilled pass catchers ever to play football. Rote's fakes were a mystery to defensive halfbacks. Lindon Crow, now an assistant coach of the Los Angeles Rams, tells of a time while he was with the Chicago Cardinals in the mid-fifties. Kyle faked him so efficiently he smashed into an official and knocked him to the ground. Crow offered apologies to the official as he picked himself up, glanced downfield at Kyle crossing the goal line, and muttered, "Now where in hell did he come from?"

THE INTERIOR LINE

I suppose we can liken a football team to a colony of bees. The coach is the ruling bee; the backs and ends who execute the glory assignments are the drones; and the linemen who perform the backbreaking assignments without much recognition are the working bees. The three units functioning together make the honey, but it's those workers up front that deserve a share of the headlines.

The Center

The center is the pivotal spot in the line. The man in that position is the first out of the huddle, and the rest of the team lines up on him. He's a guy with confident hands not likely to fumble the snap back to the quarterback. He has to have the size to take out the middle linebacker or double-team the defensive tackle. It's important, too, for him to have speed to move down under punts. His snaps have to be quick and accurate and, in the case of punts, place kicks, and extra points, must be executed almost without looking back. His move from the instant of centering the ball to the execution of his initial block must be as quick as the release of a mousetrap when the bait is nibbled. Jimmy Ringo, the Green Bay offensive captain (recently traded to Philadelphia), was everybody's choice as all-pro center last season, and rightly so. Although not the biggest lineman in the world (6 foot 1, 225 pounds), Ringo cuts down defensive tackles with brute strength and agility of motion. His angle blocking is crisp and to the point, and his intelligent moves often force the opponents to make mistakes which are costly.

The Guards

On either side of the center are the offensive guards. And all it takes to fill this position is speed, power, brains, and agility. The guard has to be big enough to move straight ahead and block out a tackle, usually larger than he is. He has to be fast enough to pull out of the line and clear a path ahead of his runner. On some plays he'll work on the defensive end or corner linebacker. On others he moves for a defensive halfback. In each instance he must keep himself between a fleet-footed ball carrier and an equally fast defensive halfback. On pass plays a guard may hit and then drop back a step to afford pass protection to his quarterback. If the defense is red-dogging,

he often has to cope with a charging middle linebacker—
that irresistible force meeting that immovable object in a
head-on collision that often causes protective equipment
to split and bodies to ache. A guard also has to move as
well to his left as he does to his right, in order to make a
team's running offense as strong to one side as it is to the
other.

Jim Parker, a seven-year veteran of the pro wars and a
member of the Baltimore Colts, is a standout at the offensive guard position. Parker is 6 foot 3, weighs 275
pounds, and doubles at the tackle spot when he's needed.
He learned his football at Ohio State, a school known for
its grinding, running game, so he's well versed on leading
the interference. Another bright performer last season
was Ken Gray of the St. Louis Cardinals, who played an
important part in the Cardinals' jump from sixth place in

1962 to third place and title contention in 1963. But the man who still rules the roost is 255-pound Jerry Kramer of the Green Bay Packers. By the time he reached his twenty-seventh birthday last year, Kramer had been hospitalized for a detached retina, an eight-inch wood splinter in his groin, several broken bones and vertebrae, a shotgun injury, and an automobile accident in which the car rolled over his body. If all this didn't stop him, how can another football player? Few do! He and "Fuzzy" Thurston, another 250-pounder, round the ends like Old 99 hauling freight down the main line. It's enough to make a defensive player double his Blue Cross!

The Tackles

Then come the offensive tackles—the brawn, the piledrivers. They too must have quick reactions and a lot of speed over the short distance. A coach may pull his tackles on certain plays, but primarily they have to do the rough blocking to bust open the holes. They're the biggest men on the line, and perhaps the roughest.

Green Bay's Forrest Gregg and New York's Roosevelt Brown were the two best last season. Both are well over 6 feet tall, and both scale in excess of 250 pounds. Brown has more speed than any big man in the league, and he's an exceptional blocker. Rosey is also a two-way man, going in on defense for the goal-line stands, and he's a respected member of the Giants' kickoff team because of his speed and sure tackling. Rosey went out for football in high school because, as he puts it, "My high school coach thought I was too big to be playing trombone in the school band!" Gregg is like a mountain of granite while pass-blocking and also fits in perfectly with Green Bay's potent running attack.

THE KICKOFF

We now know our offensive eleven and its requirements. Its objective, of course, is to score, and it begins that job with the receipt of the opening kickoff. You'll notice that a coach puts in a combination of his biggest and fastest men for the kickoff return. If these specialists can run it back all the way, they can gain a decided psychological advantage. Each team has a different method of returning the ball, and that method can change from week to week, depending on the weaknesses of the other team. But, generally speaking, you'll see that all the men except the ball carrier form a blocking pattern, trying to knock down any defender in sight. The ball carrier looks for any opening and moves toward it. The pros like to move up the middle, the basic theory being that the shortest distance between two points is a straight line. But should the ball carrier spot a defender moving, or being moved, out of the lane he's responsible for, that ball carrier will change direction and move for the highway.

It's a rather odd statistic, but the team leader in kickoff returns in 1962 and 1963 has been the Washington Redskins, although they finished fourth in the East in 1962 and sixth in 1963. And Abe Woodson of the San Francisco Forty-Niners was the individual champion for those two seasons, with an average of 31.3 and 32.2 yards respectively, although his team finished fifth in the West in 1962 and in the cellar in 1963. In 1963 there was a

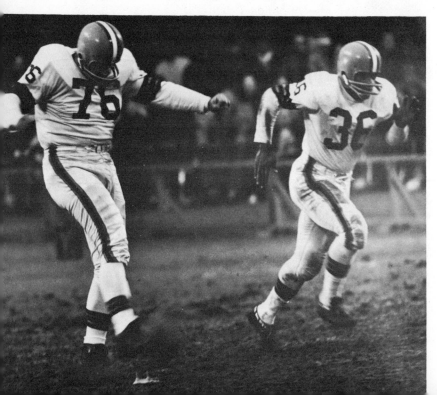

league total of only nine kickoffs returned for touchdowns, and the reason is not that the backs are slowing down, but that the defensive linemen are faster and shiftier than ever before, and are able to contain the fleet-footed deep men.

THE GAME PLAN

The offense now has the ball and is set to put the game plan into operation. For a full week before, the coaching staff and players have spent endless hours studying game films of their opponents' two previous games (a plan endorsed by all the clubs in the league). In addition, there is the scouting report, supplied in detail by the man assigned to cover the opponents' ball games. Game films and scouting reports from previous years are also brought out, and every detail of the opposition's weaknesses is studied and restudied. Nothing misses the scrutiny of the trained eye. One of the oldtimers on the opponents' club may be slowing down and vulnerable to a certain play or type of play. A rookie in another position reveals weaknesses in certain areas. Or there might be a defensive alignment susceptible to one or more of your plays. If you don't have a play for that weakness, you invent one. From all these meetings and popcornless movies comes your game plan. The quarterback's first call in the huddle is the test play—the "feeler." Its execution will allow him to spot the weaknesses in the defense and determine if the past week's lessons were well thought out.

THE BASIC OFFENSE

Watch the way the offense lines up on the line of scrimmage. Each of the teams in the NFL uses a basic "T" formation, strong to one side (see diagram), because it's the only proven offense that keeps the defense undecided between a pass or a run, until the moment of commitment. In this formation the distances between the linemen vary, depending on the type of play called and the game plan for that week. Generally there's a distance of about 30 inches between the linemen from tackle to tackle. The tight end is about 1 yard from his tackle, and the split end and flanker about 7 yards to the side of his closest man. The fullback lines up directly behind the guard on the strong (flanker) side, and the halfback positions himself directly behind the weak-side guard, and about a half-yard to the rear of his fullback. Coaches will tinker with this basic offense, using any one of a dozen or more variations.

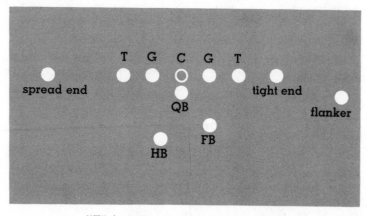

"T" formation, strong to one side

The "I" Formation

The Dallas Cowboys will frequently line up in the "I" formation, something I believe I first saw Tom Nugent's VMI team use against Army in the late forties or early fifties. Dallas uses nine different formations of the "I," so a defense may see it coming in eighteen different set-ups, when you consider they can be run to both sides. Its purpose is deception, and deception is a key word in football. In the "I" formation the quarterback is normally behind the center, the fullback is 3½ yards behind the quarterback, and the halfback is 1 yard behind the fullback. The flanker is normal, either left or right.

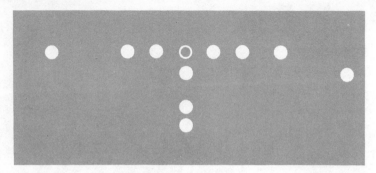

The "I" formation

Dallas will send a man in motion from this formation, or they'll use a draw play up the middle (employed in situations where the defense is red-dogging in habit sequences), or they'll shift into other formations from the "I" (of course, to throw the defense off).

The "Stacked Deck" Formation

The Philadelphia Eagles came up with another weirdie against the Giants during the 1961 season. It was called

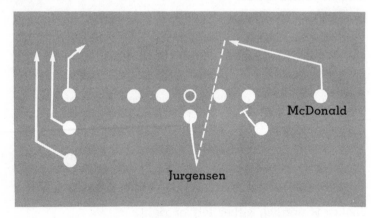

The "stacked deck" formation

the "stacked deck," and was a spread formation, primarily for passing plays, that enabled four receivers to get downfield in a hurry. In the "stacked deck," three men were sent either to the right or left and were positioned one behind the other.

Philadelphia used this play eight times against New York for a net gain of 92 yards, one of them going for a score on a 52-yard pass from Sonny Jurgensen to Tommy McDonald, the right flanker. It was also used successfully on two plays against the Detroit Lions in the final game of the season, which the Eagles won, 27–24.

MIXING THE OFFENSE

Now the quarterback will begin to mix up his plays to keep the defense off balance. If the defense is blitzing a great deal (or at least on the probable passing downs), watch for the quarterback to call the draw play instead of a pass. Here he'll jam the ball into his fullback's gut, but continue back to his pocket, as if he's setting himself for the aerial. The fullback, who has faked a pass-protection block, waits for his line to trap the fast-charging defender, and then blasts into the hole.

The Screen Pass

Another good call against a red-dogging opponent is the screen pass. This can be executed either right, left, or up the middle, depending on the weakness of the defense. Notice how the majority of quarterbacks back up for a screen pass, almost telegraphing it to the other team. Two of the tricks that make Tittle the master of the screen is the calmness with which he executes and the duplication of the motions he uses on normal pass patterns. When setting up the screen, Tittle turns his back to the opposition, completes his fakes, moves into the pocket, and then fakes the long one downfield before throwing the screen. In addition to curing the "blitz," the screen pass also fakes out the linebackers, who quickly drop back to cover receivers. This maneuver can annihilate a quarterback's long passing game, so to keep the retreating linebackers honest, the screen pass becomes an effective weapon. Being a passing quarterback, Tittle is more subjected week after week to red-dogging than most other signal-callers. Hence he gets more practice with the screen and has become the accepted best in its use.

The Cleveland Browns employ a type of screen pass designed to give their great fullback, Jimmy Brown, a running start and a couple of extra blockers. That's like adding a nuclear warhead to a nuclear warhead. They call it their 85 Flare Screen Left, a play which spreads everybody on the field. The center, a guard, and a tackle do a split-second block in the line, then move quickly across to the left. The quarterback moves straight back without faking as Brown flares out about fifteen yards to his left, moving at less than full speed, as if he weren't in the play. Further deception to draw the defense away from Brown is to send the ends and flanker running down-and-out patterns to the opposite side, pulling the defensive backs with them. By the time he's hauling the ball in, his teammates have taken out enough of the defenders to give him lots of running room, and that's like turning a kid loose in a penny-candy store with a five-dollar bill in his hand.

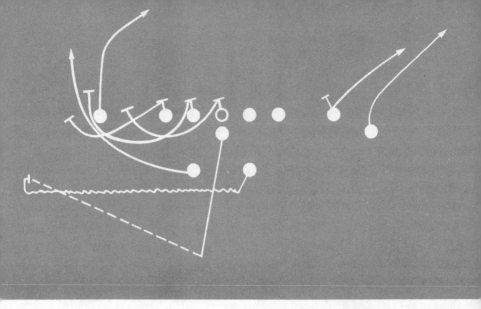

Cleveland's 85 Flare Screen Left

The Washington Redskins use a similar screen putting the setback in motion (see diagram).

The Wide Sweep

A quarterback seeing a defensive end repeatedly crash in on certain downs will invariably call a wide running play around that end. A scouting report may reveal that the end always crashes in on second down with short yardage, or on third down with long yardage. If the signal-caller has remembered his lessons, a good gain can be achieved by running wide. You at home can easily spot the wide running play by observing one or both guards, and perhaps even a tackle, pull out from their positions and run parallel to the line of scrimmage, forming the interference for the runner. Each has a definite blocking assignment, not just to knock down the first guy they see with a different-colored jersey. And you'll notice that

after executing that first block they'll be up looking for the next prospective tackler. There are times when the quarterback may spot a defensive tackle halting his charge and following the pulling guard, in order to bust up the play before any yardage can be gained. The quarterback will now try a fake sweep, with the linemen pulling as they did before, but this time the handoff goes to the other setback, who bucks into the hole left vacant by the roaming tackle.

Beating the Red-Dog

In obvious passing situations, when it's imperative to gain yardage or make up a big point difference, the quarterback knows the other team will be trying to beat him down by red-dogging. If the situation alone doesn't dictate the red-dog, his trained eye will spot the linebackers playing right on the line of scrimmage, instead of a step or two behind, and the weak-side safety man stepping in a bit closer. This is when you're likely to see a short slant pass just over the line of scrimmage, or the bomb.

The Play-Action Pass

If a team's running offense is moving well, and they're piling up yardage on the ground, a play that is often used is the play-action pass, a maneuver employed by most of the clubs in the NFL. This is a play that will never be called in an obvious passing situation, such as third down and long yardage, and, as I mentioned, it will pop up in the midst of a successful ground attack. In the Giants' final game of the 1963 season against the Steelers, the winner to clinch the Eastern crown, Y. A. Tittle exploited rookie linebacker Andy Russell for two touchdowns by using the play-action pass. On the snap from center, the quarterback fakes to his halfback, who hits inside. The tight end, meanwhile, zone-blocks the corner linebacker, to make the play look like a run. The linebacker's detainment allows the fullback to release and move out. The quarterback, following his fake to the halfback, drops back the normal 7 yards into the pocket and throws to the fullback's outside shoulder. To complete the deception, the three other receivers act as decoys, leading the defense away from the fullback, and on occasion the onside guard will pull to make the play look like a run. Timing is important on this play, and so are the fakes (see diagram on following page).

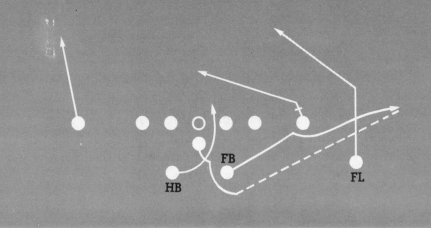

The play-action pass

THE TOUGHEST CALLS

Most quarterbacks will agree that the toughest call in football is the third-down call with long yardage required, or fourth down and one. In the first situation, most quarterbacks will pass; in the second, most will run. The defense knows this and sets for it. The action in these situations generally becomes vicious. Since trickery is a big factor in this game, and now its hand is in the open, the team with the ball has to explode more than it ordinarily would to make the play work. Technically, a coach blueprints every play to go for a touchdown, but for this actually to happen would require the biggest miracle since Glinda the Good whisked Dorothy and Toto from Oz back to their Kansas farmhouse. Yet, on that fourth-and-one play, the offense usually blocks to get more than one yard; it tries to bust through for a score. The defense, on the other hand, has a book of plays designed to stop everything it thinks the other team will throw at it. So, activity up front seethes to the boiling point.

In the third-and-long situation, the defense will usually go to a tight, man-for-man defense, and will blitz the quarterback. If a pass play is called in the huddle, the offense must fake and execute to perfection if it is going to complete the toss. Of course, there is always the possibility that the quarterback will gamble on the defense's aligning itself for the obvious and call a run in the passing situation and a pass in the running situation. The fakes and the blocks must then become the perfect execution of that perfect blueprint.

As we have said over and over, one team must adapt to the tactics of the other in order to win a ball game. A club with a dangerous, pass-catching end might find the defense double-teaming that end; that is, assigning two men to guard him, instead of the usual one. This will therefore release another potential receiver for pass-catching duties. Since the defense will pay the least attention to the one back or end least likely to be a receiver, the quarterback will call a play which sends that man into the zone (or area) vacated by the two defensive backs covering the more dangerous end. If the maneuver works, the quarterback will call the play again in a similar situation later in the game. This usually breaks up the double-team situation, which immediately tells the quarterback to fake a similar play and throw to the end whose defenders have been cut in half. If, in the course of a game, the play-by-play announcer points out the double-team, keep alert for this maneuver.

The Option Play

A team's passing game does not necessarily have to be confined to the quarterback. Some clubs have a halfback or a fullback, or both, capable of throwing the football. This creates an added woe for the defense. The offense will build a series of plays to take advantage of its backs' versatility. They're called option plays, and, as the term implies, the back has the choice of either running or passing the ball, depending on how the defense reacts to his moves. On the option, the quarterback takes the snap from center and tosses the ball to the deep back, who begins what appears to be an end run. The weak-side guard will pull out and run interference, along with the other back, while the other guard, the center, and the two tackles block for a running play. The two ends and the flanker may fake a block, but they move downfield in definite pass-patterns. If one of them can shake free, the back with the ball will pass to him. If there are no open receivers, the back will take a tighter grip on the ball and run with it (see diagram).

The pros don't usually like to run their quarterbacks, because of the danger of injury to their key man, but once in a while a Tittle or a Starr or a Johnson will keep the defense honest by calling a quarterback option play. Here he'll spin, fake a handoff, and then roll out to the side. If

The option play

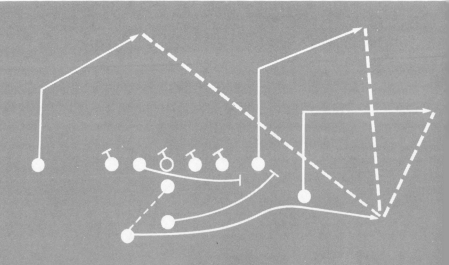

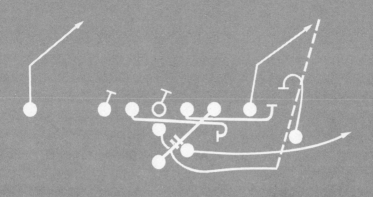

Green Bay's quarterback option play

the way is clear, he'll run. If a receiver is free, he'll pass. Green Bay's quarterback option is illustrated in the diagram.

The Bootleg

Another deceptive play to watch for is the quarterback bootleg. Here the quarterback tries to give the impression he has handed off, when all the time he continues his motion, concealing the ball along the side of his thigh away from the defenders' line of vision. From this position the quarterback can either run or pass. Y. A. Tittle employs the bootleg from time to time. In fact, in a November 1963 game against the Forty-Niners, the play threw the game into a rout. The Giants' bootleg formation has Tittle faking to his halfback (who crashes to the weak side of the center). He then rolls to his left with the ball clutched in one hand and resting against his thigh. Both ends and the flanker back also move in patterns to the left, drawing the defense with them. The remaining back, meanwhile, brush-blocks and then moves downfield slowly to his right. At the last instant, Tittle

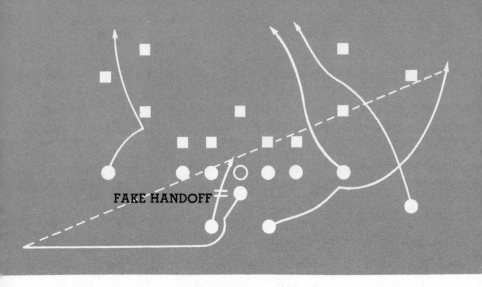

FAKE HANDOFF

The Giants' bootleg play

stops, wheels, and throws to the opposite side, a difficult maneuver, when you consider that Tittle was moving to his left, and is a right-handed passer. In the San Francisco game, the play was good for 45 yards and a touchdown (see diagram).

Combating the Zone Defense

Quarterbacks confronted with a zone, rather than a man-to-man, pass defense will change their tactics to take advantage of areas left uncovered by the zone arrangement. The secret of penetrating a zone defense seems to lie in the ability of the quarterback to call a play which will take a defensive man out of his zone, even for an instant. This is done by faking to certain areas and then striking in the cleared-out areas. If, for example, you can draw your middle linebacker straight back and the corner linebacker toward the sideline, you create an open area which is conceivably open for the tight end or the flanker back for a quick pass. A tight end, moving down to his left, and a fullback, moving out to the right flat, could allow the flanker to go down and then into the empty area. The basic rule for a defender in a zone defense is not to leave that zone. The basic rule for a quarterback facing a zone defense is to fake the defender out of his zone. Whoever wins that mental battle will generally win the game.

THE RUNNING GAME

While the pass has become the most effective striking force of the pro offense and the simplest way of combating those thousand-pound forward walls, the running game should not be neglected. Since football is played in any weather, it's possible that the elements will not allow for an effective passing game. A wet ball cannot always be controlled, and the offense is not anxious to let the other team get its hands on it, so the offense sticks to the ground. The running game is also used to keep the defense off balance, particularly when you have fast, powerful backs who are capable of penetrating those aggressive line-backers. The Packers and the Browns are the two teams who can kill you on the ground. So will the Steelers. They love the power plays, the carry-overs from the old-fashioned single-wing days, and they have the personnel, both up front and in the backfield, to mow you down on almost every play. And when those defenders get weary from the steady pounding, they'll hit you with that unexpected pass play for long yardage.

Some coaches believe you can't get hurt when the other team sticks primarily to the ground, and they cite statistics to prove it. Cleveland, for example, gained over 2600 yards on the ground in 1963 to lead the league in that department, yet had to settle for second place in the Eastern Conference. The Giants, on the other hand, could muster only 1777 yards on the ground, but passed for 3247 and the Eastern title. However, my memory takes me back to the 1961 championship game between New York and Green Bay, which the Packers won 37–0. True, Bart Starr hit on three touchdown passes, but they were set up by his calling 44 running plays, compared to the Giants' 14. Starr threw only 19 passes, compared to Tittle's 29.

There's no big secret to a successful running game. For short yardage you use the straight power play, with lots of double-teaming (two offensive linemen moving out one defensive tackle, and a guard pulling to join with his fullback in moving out the defensive end) while your halfback busts up the tackle hole. Variations, of course, have the fullback moving inside the guard, with the center moving ahead for the middle linebacker and the offensive guard moving the defensive tackle to the outside. For longer yardage, you use your end runs. Up the middle, off-tackle, or around the ends—those are basic. What makes them effective are the variations and the fakes, and a coach will devise as many as there are defensive weaknesses. An end run generally commands lots of room to the outside, so to take advantage of the defense that anticipates the wide run, a quarterback will occasionally sweep to the side with less running room. In this situation, of course, one of the backs must fake going to the wide open spaces to confuse the defense, while the other

back takes the ball and moves to the smaller area. This is a play, though, that requires an extra effort on the part of the weak-side blockers, who get no double-team help but must work man-for-man.

INSIDE THE TEN-YARD LINE

One area where the going gets toughest is inside the ten-yard line. First down, and goal to go! In this situation the offense has four downs in which to score or give up the ball to the other side. You can be sure the other side will do everything in its power to prevent the score and get the ball back. The ace-in-the-hole weapon, of course, is the field goal. Except in cases where the kick is blocked, a professional doesn't usually miss his target at this distance, so a team is almost assured of three points at this point. But it's nicer to have six (which almost automatically gives you seven, since the kicker rarely misses the extra-point attempt), so you spend at least three of your four downs in trying for the touchdown. Then, too, three points might not do your cause any good —you may be forced to use all four downs in an effort to score, and perhaps even win the game.

When you're inside the ten, you have less than twenty yards (including the end zone) in which to maneuver, so your position eliminates all your long passing plays. You run quick power plays, with lots of trapping, and you sweep wide. You pass to the flat, or try quick pops over the middle, or you use the screen. You look for patterns

in your repertoire which might allow you to use the goal posts to your advantage; that is, to put the goal posts between the defender and your receiver. If the first two plays don't produce the touchdown, the quarterback will probably call a third-down play designed to score. If it fails, the ball is still in good position for the field-goal attempt.

AUTOMATICS

As you know, the offense lines up for the huddle about ten yards behind the line of scrimmage, so that the defense can't overhear the call. Thirty seconds are allowed back there, so judgments must be quick. When the team returns to the line of scrimmage, the quarterback sizes up the defense to determine whether or not the play called in the huddle will work against the defensive alignment. If not, he'll call a new play at the line of scrimmage. These are referred to as "automatics," or "audibles," or "check-signals." I've known some quarterbacks to call as many as thirty or forty "automatics" in the fifty to sixty times they had the ball in a game. Some teams use numbers for their automatic signals; others use colors. Both work the same way. All plays in the National Football League are designed to be run against a 4–3 defense, since this is the one most commonly used. There is one column of plays which demand that a lineman be able to run against every defense. A second column of plays is designed for certain defenses. The "automatics," of course, are chosen from that list of plays which can be run against any defense.

Say, in the huddle, the quarterback calls "29 pitchout on 3." "29 pitchout" is the play designated; "3" is the number on which the center will snap the ball. The team lines up on the line of scrimmage, and the quarterback decides the play can't work against the present defense. He will then shout, "Three," the repeat of the snap signal, to tell his teammates that a change is coming; this to be followed by a new play number, say "86." "THREE—86." Since the defenders don't know the original snap number, they don't know when they hear the audible if the play will begin on three, or if the quarterback's call on the line was a fake. Often, if the call in the huddle is not to change, the quarterback will shout a phony signal at the line to confuse the defense. His team, hearing a number other than the one called in the huddle, will pay no attention to the new call.

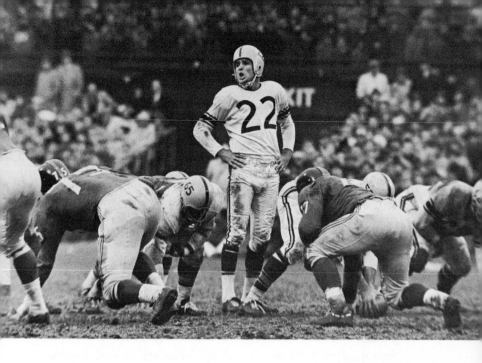

Some teams, as I said, use colors instead of numbers for their automatics. In the huddle, for example, the play may be "34 on 4." If the play is to be changed at the line of scrimmage, a pre-designated color indicating the same snap number will be called by the quarterback at the line. If the code color is "green," "34 on 4" could become "Green—49" at the line of scrimmage, "GREEN" indicating the change is to take place with the snap signal remaining "4," and "49" indicating the new play. Teams generally change their automatics with each new appearance on the field. Thus, automatics are apt to take on several new meanings throughout a game. Y. A. Tittle has a favorite trick of calling the same "automatic" three times during the first three quarters of a ball game, each play executed exactly the same way. Then, in the fourth quarter, he calls the same "automatic" number, but this time with a new meaning altogether.

THE LAST TWO MINUTES

A throbbing climax to a tight football game is the scoring attempt in the final two minutes of action. The best example in many a year came in the closing moments of the 1963 Army-Navy game. Ranked second in the nation, with its only loss coming via the upset route to Southern Methodist, the Middies led underdog Army 21–15, but their backs were to the goal line and there was still time for the Cadets to score. The 100,000 spectators boiled over, despite the December chill, and many blame the roar of the crowd for Army's failure to produce a game-tying touchdown. After nearly 13½ minutes of the final quarter, the Cadets had rallied to within striking distance. Carl Stichweh, Ken Waldrop, and Ray Paske alternated at running and passing as the Army forward wall ripped the Navy defense to shreds. The clock read 1:38. The noise was deafening. Quarterback Stichweh held his arms high in an appeal for quiet and even had to use a precious time-out to stop the clock. It was first down, the ball on the Navy seven. Paske plowed in to the five. The clock continued. Then Waldrop bulled in to the four. The seconds ticked. Again Waldrop plunged into the line, this time to the two. Stichweh, in a frenzy with time running out, again raised his arms and asked for quiet—screamed for a time out—but the howling crowd absorbed his plea. The gun sounded, and Navy had won.

Some fans said the officials were to blame for not calling a time-out until order was maintained. Others blamed the Army players for not using their available downs to better advantage. But Army's great coach, Paul Dietzel, exonerated the officials from any blame. He also pointed out the coolness of his quarterback. "If anyone's to blame," said Dietzel in a Monday-morning-quarterback session, "it's me for not being more fully aware of just what the rules are." Dietzel added that there were eight seconds remaining in the game to get in that fourth-down play, but by the time Stichweh and the team were lined up and Stichweh's signals could be heard, time had run out.

The college rules state that a quarterback can request an official to stop the clock if his signals can't be heard because of excess crowd noise. The referee has the power to act upon this request if he deems it legitimate. Both Stichweh and the referee (Barney Finn) acted properly in this situation, so Dietzel was just being the big man everyone knows him to be, by taking the pressure off a responsible official and a broken-hearted football team. I'm certain the 1964 spring football practice sessions on the plains of West Point included many drills where the offense had fourth down and goal to go, with eight seconds remaining. And I'll bet that the offense "scored" 99 per cent of the time.

The pros spend a lot of time in each week's practice session trying to score from various positions on the field with just two minutes remaining. Every minute the offense has the ball, there is an opportunity to score, and the pros have, at times, scored two and three times with less than two minutes remaining in a ball game. When there are a lot of yards to eat up, the long pass, known as "the bomb," is often used. Here it's a matter of the split end or the flanker beating out the defender. He tears straight down the field, as the quarterback sets and then lofts the arcing spiral to a definite predetermined spot on the field. If the intended receiver can win the race and hold onto the ball, it can mean the difference in the outcome of the game. If the defense is double-teaming the other club's dangerous receiver, a quarterback will go with his short- and medium-range passes, usually throwing toward the sidelines to avoid interceptions and to give the receiver the opportunity to step out of bounds and stop the clock.

Intentionally grounding the football (that is, passing the ball, in an effort to stop the clock, to an area where there is obviously no receiver) draws a penalty, so the pros often devise methods to avoid precious loss of time and yards. Several times I have seen a team, frantic to get in another play before the gun goes off, line up without benefit of a huddle. By prearranged signal, the ball is quickly snapped, the quarterback races back his 7 yards and throws a high bullet out of the reach of any intercepters and just out of reach of a receiver who has conveniently positioned himself at the sideline boundary marker. The clock is stopped, and the offense has that extra moment to develop a scoring strategy.

Because the pros play two-platoon football (one group playing only on offense; the other only on defense, with other specialized teams going in for kickoffs, kickoff returns, punts, and the like), the players get many opportunities to "rest" during a game, so it's not necessary to use any time-outs for fifty-eight of the sixty playing minutes. Time-outs can be used to better strategic advantage in those final two minutes to stop the clock after a running play, or in any other critical moment where time is essential. (Each team is allowed three charged time-outs per half without penalty.) So when you see your quarterback throw out-of-bounds in the last two minutes and miss his receiver by two yards, don't call him a bum. He may have just executed his best play of the game.

THE PUNT

One of the most important weapons a football team owns is the punt. A sputtering offense, unable to make the first down and deep in its own territory, can put itself back in the ball game merely by giving the ball a 40- to 70-yard "ride" downfield and away from the goal it is defending. That chore is in the hands (or, more properly, the foot) of the kicking specialist. Every team in the National Football League has at least one. He can stand fourteen yards behind his own center and, with icy calm, ignore perhaps two or three kick-blocking experts, as his foot meets the ball and sends it spiraling through the air. Detroit's Yale Lary led the NFL in 1963 with an average distance of 48.9 yards (or about 63 yards from the point the ball was booted) without a single blocked kick. This kind of skill has at times been responsible for winning a game that might otherwise have gone the other way.

In a 1959 game between the New York Giants and the Cleveland Browns at Cleveland, the Giants' Don Chandler kicked eight times, five of them into a stiff wind, and yet averaged 54 yards per kick. He punted 47 yards out of bounds on the Cleveland four. The next went 56 yards and out of bounds on the Cleveland six. A boot of 43 yards again went out of bounds on the Cleveland four. Then came a mighty blast of 62 yards that traveled into the end zone. Another of 53 yards sailed into the end zone. And, finally, a 43-yard kick went out of bounds on the Brown's thirty. This display of punting distance and accuracy was responsible for keeping Cleveland in a hole all afternoon, and the Giants won the ball game.

There are a number of things you can watch for in a punting situation. First, if fourth down and long yardage aren't enough to convince you a kick is forthcoming, your television screen will supply undisputed evidence, as you see both offense and defense send in their special punting and punt-return teams. The field suddenly looks like an ant colony at a Sunday picnic.

It takes less than two and a half seconds from the time the center snaps the ball until it leaves the kicker's foot, so you'll have to look quickly. (A team averages about six punts per game, though, so you'll have a dozen occasions to spot the various techniques employed by the kicking team.)

The Center in Punt Formation

In punt formation, the center is a key man. His snap has to be quick and accurate. If an opposing lineman is playing directly in front of him, he has the added responsibility of throwing a block. If the way ahead is clear, he'll be the first man out of the line to cover the punt return. Some centers will take their stance over the ball, look back through their legs at the kicker, look up at the defensive alignment, look back again through their legs at the kicker, and then snap the ball on the signal. This can sometimes be suicidal, since a defender is very apt to wait until the center has completed his logistics and then move directly in front of him while he gazes back at his kicker. Some centers, like Ray Wietecha (formerly of the Giants and now an assistant coach of the Los Angeles Rams) and Greg Larson (a converted guard and number 53 on the Giants' roster), have developed the technique of centering the ball straight back without looking at the kicker a second time, thus alerting them-

selves to any changes in the defense. This takes a great deal of practice and skill, but it can save a center from a bruising afternoon at the hands of an unfriendly lineman or linebacker. The top centers in the league can even send the ball back so that the laces are exactly where the punter wants them: on top. Even a Houdini has to blink twice at that trick.

Protecting the Kicker

In those two and a half seconds between the time the center snaps the ball and the actual kick, there are some pretty solid collisions "up front." Teams vary in their methods, depending on the skills of their personnel, but generally speaking, late in the game and with the ball deep in enemy territory, the defense will be trying to rush the punter and block the kick. The offensive line, therefore, tightens up from tackle to tackle and does its best to plug the gaps and keep everything bottled up in the middle. The ends will block, or brush-block, on occasion, but their prime duty is to move downfield to cover.

Two of the three blocking backs will line up approximately one yard behind the front line, and each will position himself outside his tackle. Their job is to look to the outside, to delay the onrushing defense by blocking it away from the kicker, to keep the longest distance between two points a curved line. The third blocking back, known as the deep blocker (the Green Bay Packers' head coach, Vince Lombardi, calls him the "personal interferer"), is equidistant from the center and the punter and must pick off anyone leaking through. If more than one of his teammates fails in his assignment, the "personal interferer" gets interfered with—but good!

If everyone performs the way the coaching staff has diagramed the play on the blackboard, the kicker "gets it away" and immediately becomes one of two safety men. The deep blocker is the other, and each is responsible for a side. This automatically tells you that, in addition to the specialized skill of being able to boot the ball high and far, the kicker must also possess speed and be an adept tackler.

The Kicker

Once you've diagnosed what's going on in the line, turn your attention to the kicker. His years of experience have made his moves almost machine-like. Most punters in the league use one and a half steps in their kicking motion; that is, they stand with the kicking foot slightly back as the ball is caught. The kicking foot then comes forward one-half step, followed by a full step with the other foot, and then the kick. The Giants' Don Chandler is an exception; he uses three steps, and will take one of them as the ball sails toward his outstretched hands. Chandler also has an unorthodox manner of holding the ball on top before it's dropped, while the majority of punters hold the ball on the side and underneath. But Chandler's distance and accuracy are unquestioned, so no coach would ever bother to go back to book fundamentals in his case.

The Fake Kick

A kicker with speed gives you one more thing to watch for: a run from punt formation. Be alert for this play if the offense is past its own forty-yard line and can afford to gamble. If a run is called from punt formation, the other backs will form a wall of protection in front of the kicker-turned-runner, and the play will generally sweep one of the ends where there's more room to operate.

One sure way of spotting a fake-kick, pass situation is to watch the center, as well as the other linemen, from tackle to tackle. Since they are ineligible receivers, they won't leave the line of scrimmage in a passing situation, whereas, if a punt has been called in the huddle, they'll be moving downfield almost immediately.

Returning the Kick

In a punting situation, the defense will predetermine its strategy. Generally the team without a speedy breakaway runner will attempt to block a punt, and, if that's not successful, call for the fair catch. Those teams equipped with a back who can run the hundred in under ten seconds and shift directions quicker than a woman driver will drop their front men back and form a wall of protection for "Mercury."

The receiving team usually has two men back, one on either side. While the ball is in flight, the back farthest away shouts out whether or not the fair catch should be called. This split-second decision is determined by how fast the kicking team covers the punt. If the back feels they can run, he alerts the receiver and immediately becomes the ball carrier's blocker. Most teams run the punt back either left or right, seldom up the middle where most of the traffic is. The blocking pattern is set up to take the play all the way, but the guys on the kicking team are in there for a reason; they're fast, aggressive, and brutal tacklers. A punt is seldom returned for a touchdown. In fact, during the entire fourteen-game schedule of each team in the National Football League during the 1963 season (a total of ninety-eight games) only Abe Woodson of the San Francisco Forty-Niners accomplished the feat, going 85 yards, much to the embarrassment of the world champion Green Bay Packers.

THE FIELD GOAL

Even more specialized than the punt is the field goal. The kicker must drop-kick or place-kick the ball over the horizontal bar of the goal post, and within an 18½-foot

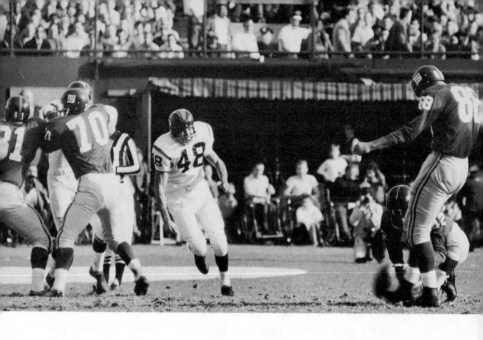

corridor between the vertical posts. Often the "magic toe" has to contend with a bad angle or a stiff wind, in addition to the onslaught of the defense. Yet the field-goal kicker has become so skilled he is often found among the top five scorers in the league. Pittsburgh's Lou Michaels, for example, threw his 235 pounds into 26 field goals in 1962, and, with his 32 extra points, finished second in scoring with 110 points, the most ever scored in one season on kicking alone. Don Chandler of the Giants was the individual scoring champion for 1963. He kicked 18 field goals and 52 extra points for a total of 106 points.

A peek into the past reveals that quite a few world-championship games in the National Football League were decided by the field-goal kicker. In the first title game, played in 1933 before 26,000 fans at Chicago's Wrigley Field, the Bears' "Automatic" Jack Manders kicked three field goals and two extra points to help edge New York, 23–21. More recently the Green Bay Packers won the crown in 1962, defeating the Giants 16–7. That 9-point difference was supplied by Jerry Kramer's three field goals, kicked in swirling thirty-mile-per-hour winds.

Any time the offense is within fifty yards of the goal line, you're apt to see a field goal attempted. One way the viewer can "call" the field goal is to determine whether the three points will do the team any good. A simpler way, of course, is to note the arrival of the holder and the kicker. These two, along with the center, become the key figures in the field-goal attempt. Here again, the more proficient centers in the league will snap the ball to the holder without looking back a second time. The laces will be exactly where the holder wants them—away from the kicker—and the ball will travel low and fast.

You will notice that the holder is almost invariably a quarterback, for at least two reasons. First, he is most used to handling the ball and is less apt to fumble the snap from center. Second, in the event of a fake kick, the quarterback can be best depended upon to throw a forward pass.

The Fake Field Goal

After a team has lined up for a field-goal attempt, note in your mind who the eligible receivers are, in the event the play is a fake. Most often, in the fake-field-goal pass pattern, the end on the side the quarterback has run to will go deep, down, and out; the blocking back will go shallow, also down and out; while the opposite end will run down and across. The play has often worked since the element of surprise is always on the side of the offense. Variations of the fake field goal are found in the dusty files of a coach's brain. One such play was successfully

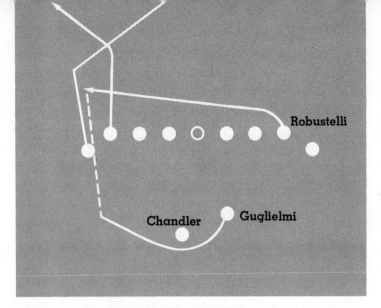

Robustelli's fake field goal

used by the Giants against the St. Louis Cardinals on November 4, 1962. A sell-out crowd at Yankee Stadium went into a fourth-quarter frenzy when Andy Robustelli, a twelve-year defensive specialist, caught a pass for a key first down from Ralph Guglielmi, following what looked, at first glance, to be a field-goal attempt.

CONCLUSION

It is not possible to cover all the situations which the offense might encounter in a football game. I have attempted to highlight the most frequent plays and occurrences. Remember that a team has four downs to gain ten yards, or else it surrenders the ball to the other side. Play sequences deep in your own territory will naturally differ from those called deep in the enemy territory. If a team doesn't make a first down in its first three downs, and it's back of midfield, you can expect a punt. If it's beyond midfield—and certainly if it's past the other team's thirty-five—you're likely to see the field-goal attempt, assuming that three points would be helpful to the offense. Inside the enemy's twenty, with fourth down and little yardage, look for a running play. If the offense doesn't make the first down, and has to surrender the ball, the other team still has a long way to go to do damage. And any time a team has gone beyond its own thirty-five-yard line, you can expect the long pass on any down, in almost any situation.

Now we know a good deal about the eleven men who know exactly where each play is going on each down, the eleven men who have the advantage of surprise on their side whenever they have the ball, the men who make the points. Let's learn a bit about the eleven men who never know where the play is going until the moment of execution, but the eleven men without whom you could never win a ball game—the defense.

3. Defense

In the absence of curvy cheerleaders with short skirts the best morale-builder a professional team can have is its defensive unit. It gets you the ball back!

On one Sunday afternoon not too long ago I stood by as a defensive coach addressed his players. They had just lost the toss of the coin and were forced to kick off. The coach clenched both fists and ground out his words. "I want you to move down that field like lightning. I want that ball carrier bounced back five yards when he's hit, and I want that ball popping out of his hands. Get that ball, and make 'em spit cider!" The speech had its effect. The ball carrier caught the ball on his five-yard line, dodged and faked his way back to the eighteen, and was promptly hit high, low, and in the middle at the same time. The ball squirted from his grasp and was instantly pounced upon by a member of the kicking team who was either alert or particularly impressed by his coach's speech of a few moments before. The ball carrier limped slowly off the field, perhaps thinking about the current market price for cider.

This type of ferocity is typical of defensive ball players. They thrive on bodily contact. In the case of a running play, it's their job to get the ball carrier and haul him down. And before they can lay their hands on the ball carrier, they must beat the offensive blockers. In the event of a pass play, they go for the passer with no expression of endearment whatsoever. At times it looks as if they're trying to take the passer's most precious weapon from him—his arm. Defensive linemen never know what's going to happen next; they can't commit themselves until that split second following the snap of the ball. Because they have this disadvantage, the defensive players are permitted by official rules to use their hands and arms to aid their cause. In the frenzy of action on the front line, the use of hands and arms sometimes gives the impression of dirty play to viewers at home. I can't say illegal maneuvers are never performed on a field during the course of a football game, because the whistles of the officials often prove the contrary. But I think I'm safe in saying that most of the play is within the rules. Professional football players respect one another and are fully aware of their responsibilities to the public paying their salaries. They don't want to jeopardize their livelihoods with a serious infraction. The rules provide for enough contact without their having to add any extras on their own.

IMPORTANCE OF THE DEFENSIVE UNIT

Defensive teams have become so specialized and so colorful, they sometimes garner more respect and adulation from the fans than do the so-called glory boys on offense. Yankee Stadium rumbles with cheers and applause when the defense is introduced before the ball game; acclaim for the offensive stars is much less audible. And of late defensive teams have been the key to victory. In 1963 the Chicago Bears won the Western Conference title with an almost incredible record of eleven wins, only one loss (an upset to Philadelphia), and two ties (Pittsburgh and Minnesota). Yet they were tenth in the fourteen-team league in total point scoring. The significant statistic is in the defensive column: the Bears allowed only 144 points to be scored against them all year. The next closest figure, 206 points, belonged to the Green Bay Packers, who finished second in the West, their only two losses coming at the hands of the Bears.

PUTTING THE PRESSURE
ON THE PASSER

Chicago met the Giants for the world championship on December 29, 1963, on freezing Wrigley Field, and it was the bone-crunching game everyone expected. But it was the Bears' defense that won out. A Tittle-to-Gifford pass with a little more than seven minutes gone in the first quarter, followed by Don Chandler's conversion, put New York out in front, 7–0, and Giant fans watching on TV were collecting their bets. The Chicago defense, however, had reaffirmed what they had learned in practice the week before: the only way to stop the Giant offense was to stop Tittle.

Doug Atkins, the 6-foot, 9-inch defensive end who was to be on Tittle's back most of the afternoon, joined by linebackers Joe Fortunato and Larry Morris (another 455 pounds) combined their momentum to bend Tittle in half. Ligaments tore in the quarterback's left knee, and

he was helped to the dressing room. Tittle returned in
the second half, his knee heavily bandaged and injected
with pain-killers and cortisone. His effectiveness waned,
and the relentless Chicago defense wouldn't let up. Then
came the turning point. The Giants had first and ten on
the Bears' thirty-one. Tittle threw the bomb to Del Shofner, who had outraced Dave Whitsell into the end zone,
but the ball bounced off his fingertips. Now, second and
ten, Tittle reached for his ace-in-the-hole, the screen pass,
the play which he had made so effective throughout the
year. The Giants lined up strong right. Tittle rolled in
that direction, looking quickly for his fullback, Joe Morrison. Morrison wasn't looking at the instant Y. A. was
ready to throw. He looked the other way and threw to

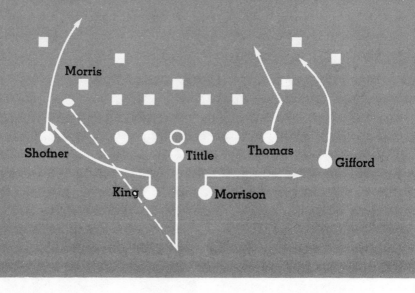

Chicago's interception of Tittle's screen pass

Phil King, his halfback. But by this time Doug Atkins had crashed through and bombarded Tittle as the ball was released. The alert Larry Morris intercepted and raced into the clear down the right sideline. As he moved past the stunned Giant bench, one of his own defensive halfbacks, Roosevelt Taylor, screamed for a lateral, but Morris kept the ball and lumbered all the way to the Giants' five. One play later, Bill Wade was in for a score. Ed O'Bradovich made another important interception in the third quarter, setting up the Bears' winning touchdown, but it was that first theft which gave the Bears the inspiration they needed to win (see diagram).

The Thanksgiving Day game in 1962 was another example of defense crushing offense. Destiny was to take the Green Bay Packers to a conference crown and a world championship, but they were to lose one game in 1962, and that loss came on November 22. Detroit's supercharged front four, Alex Karras, Roger Brown, Sam Williams, and Darris McCord, put together the best-joined effort that 57,000 fans in Tiger Stadium and many millions watching on television ever saw. They made Swiss cheese of the Packers' forward wall and had Bart Starr eating dirt so often the Green Bay quarterback thought he was a mole. Linebackers Joe Schmidt (perhaps the best ever to put on a football uniform), Wayne Walker, and Carl Brettschneider alternated in the rushing scheme to the point of frustration, and still another frustration to Green Bay was the Lions' complete reversal of their secondary pass defense from the method they used earlier in the year. Detroit's defense was just too overpowering that afternoon. The Lions won the game, 26–14.

PREPARING THE DEFENSE

All coaches plan their offenses to adapt to the talents of their personnel. At the same time they plot offensive strategy which they feel will surprise the defense. It doesn't take too long, however, for the defenses to catch up. In preparing for the 1964 New Year's Day Cotton Bowl Game, Darrell Royal, the Texas coach, geared his offense to the type of defenses he knew Navy employed in their regular season. But the first time the Longhorns got the ball, they found Navy in almost an eight-man line designed to stop the Texas ground game. Royal ordered a long-passing game, and Texas scored. Moments later, they scored again in the same fashion. Navy coach Wayne Hardin readjusted his defenses, but the damage had already been done. The Navy could never recover.

It may sound after the fact, but Hardin said later he never figured Texas for a passing game. If he had to play them again, however, he would adjust *his* defenses to cover all phases of the running and passing game.

THE BASIC DEFENSE

The pros use many offensive variations, but the basic one, as we have said, is the split "T," with a flanker either right or left. They have also figured out through experience that the best defense against this formation is the 4–3, with four slabs of beef up front, three more a step behind, and the four remaining rangy, speedy backs arranged in what sometimes is referred to as the "umbrella secondary" (see diagram).

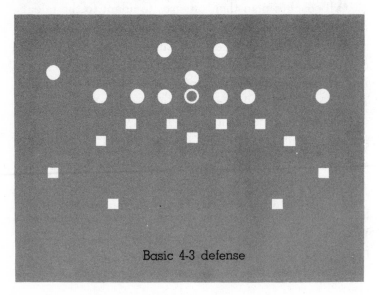

Basic 4-3 defense

THE ENDS

Let's look first at the front four, comprised of two defensive ends on the outside and two defensive tackles on the inside. While the defensive end is the outside man on the line of scrimmage, the corner linebackers are usually so close behind and slightly more to the outside that he actually serves as a defensive tackle rather than an end. He's also playing opposite the offensive tackle, or just to his outside shoulder, so he must have the size to cope with the brute force he's sure to feel, play after play. His reflexes must be tiger-like. He knows the offensive guard often pulls and charges low along the line of scrimmage with one purpose: to cut him down. He must be alert for the "trap." His usual tipoff: the offensive tackle blocking to the inside after brush-blocking the defensive end.

As an integral member of the rushing team, the defensive end must withstand double-teaming or the trap to get to the quarterback and stop him from throwing the ball. By prearranged signal with his teammates, he may charge inside, outside, or straight over the line, but he won't give up until his hands are on the quarterback, or the whistle blows the play dead. Since the defense is allowed to use hands and arms, and because it's up front where the real rough work takes place, notice how the defensive end will grip a tackle and jerk him down. Notice, too, his pursuit of the quarterback; he never forgets the old adage, "The only way to stop the passing game is to stop the passer." As he nears the thrower, he'll do his utmost to obscure the passer's vision with arm-waving tactics, and then his last lunge will be for the quarterback's arm and head. Sure it's rough, but that's the synonym for football.

Gino Marchetti of the Baltimore Colts, a twelve-year veteran of the pro football wars, has been an all-pro defensive end for the last eight seasons. The reasons are not only his speed and strength, but his brains. Marchetti keys on certain players, studies them intently. He has learned to "read" the opposition, knows the bad habits of opposing linemen. A slight change in the position of the other guy's foot, or a quick glance of his eye, or a certain way of leaning might tell Marchetti where the next play is going. His reactions to the opposition's moves are swift, and he's a tough man to trap. If Gino has any shortcomings at all, they lie in his own philosophy that no team in the NFL can win by running the ball. He therefore plays 90 per cent of the plays with the thought that the other team is going to pass. Marchetti's blistering line play in the 1958 championship game, tagged as one of the all-time greatest, sent the game into an overtime period and helped give the Colts a 23–17 victory over the Giants.

Viewers this past season also got a good taste of another pair of great defensive ends—Chicago's Doug Atkins and New York's Jim Katcavage. These two hard-nose guys are expert at keeping everything inside, one of the key responsibilities of their position. It's a rare occasion when a runner gets to the outside of either.

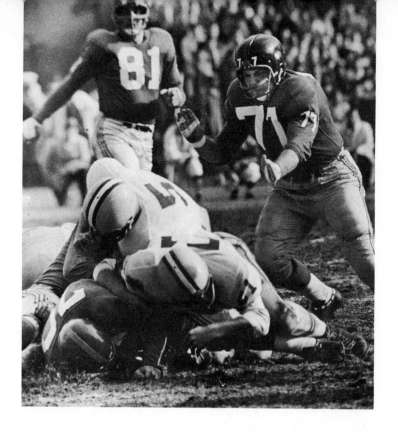

THE TACKLES

The inside men, the tackles, are the biggest and toughest men on the front line. They have to be. They're up against the two largest men on the offensive side, and they're frequently double-teamed or trapped. They've got to have the strength of two men, be quick and strong with their hands, and fast enough to pursue the quarter-back in his pocket, or the swift-footed halfback sweeping for the outside. On goal-line stands, they brace for the beating. They must repel with sure-footed force, and they must tackle crisply and with certainty.

Tackles generally key on the offensive guards, looking for the tip-off and the bad habits. Two of the better dissecters working as a unit are Green Bay's Henry Jordan and Dave Hanner; Jordan, 6 foot 3, 250 pounds; Hanner, 6 foot 2, 260 pounds. The two together are the key to Green Bay's solid defense. Don't get 'em angry. They're rough enough playing within the rules. Jordan was a heavyweight wrestler at the University of Virginia and made the NCAA finals in 1957. For the past four of his seven years in the NFL, he's been everyone's all-pro tackle. With his wrestling background, it's easy to see how he moves the enemy around like so many toys.

Hanner is a soil conservationist in the off-season, which probably explains why he's so reluctant to give ground to the other side. Nicknamed "Hawg," he's one animal who will never get slaughtered.

With Alex Karras sitting out a one-year suspension last season, Detroit's Roger Brown came into his own as one of the great defensive linemen. Brown is 6 foot 5 and weighs 300 pounds but has overwhelming speed for his bulk. In fact, in the seven or eight yards he travels to get the passer, or the ten to twenty yards he covers to pursue a ball carrier, Brown rivals any track star. Many quarterbacks who have had a full afternoon of Roger Brown spend several days in the whirlpool baths and under diathermy machines to try to forget. It's not easy.

"The Fearsome Foursome"

When the time comes for me to tell my grandchildren about the four men up front, however, I believe I'll always

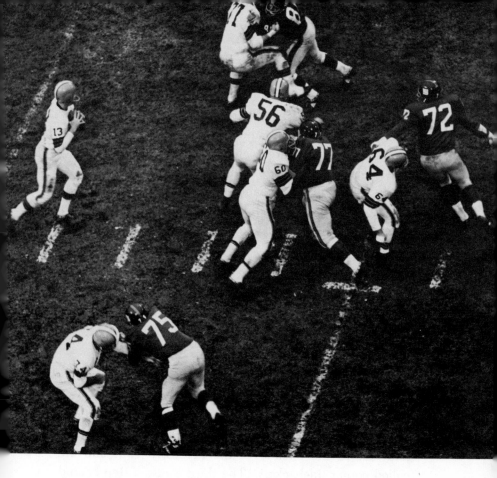

be partial to the Giants' quartet which became known as the "Fearsome Foursome." Jim Katcavage and Andy Robustelli were the ends; Dick Modzelewski and Roosevelt Grier, the tackles. More than a thousand pounds of combined weight, they began their cooperative effort of destroying enemy offense back in 1956, and played as a unit until Grier was traded to the Los Angeles Rams in July of 1963.

During the period they were together, Modzelewski, Robustelli, and Grier were never sidelined by injuries. A shoulder separation kept Katcavage out of four games in

1960, the only year from 1958 through 1963 that the Giants did not win the Eastern title. Their exploits number in the thousands, and even fans outside of New York rose to cheer them on many occasions. In 1964 Robustelli ended his playing career and "Mighty Mo" was traded to Cleveland. New faces will line up alongside Jim Katcavage, and, with the Giants' spirit, the new quartet will undoubtedly perform well, but no one will ever take the place of the "Fearsome Foursome."

THE LINEBACKERS

The linebackers form the second line of defense and consequently are known as the secondary. In the basic 4–3 alignment, two of the trio are positioned a step behind and just to the outside of the defensive ends and are called corner linebackers. The third is also a step behind his front four and lines up on the head of the offensive center. He's the middle linebacker.

A linebacker can be the busiest guy on a football team. He must be alert for the blockers, the runners, and the pass receivers. He's got to be big, fast, aggressive, and an expert tackler. On one play he may be red-dogging; on the next, he may be backing up to knock down a forward pass; on still another, he may be called upon to stop a 230-pound fullback for no gain at the line of scrimmage. It's a most demanding position and requires a lot of brainpower as well as speed and brawn. Because they must

rove a great deal to cover open gaps, the linebackers are usually in the middle of, or right near, every play of the ball game.

Joe Schmidt of the Detroit Lions is the acknowledged best middle linebacker, perhaps of all time. A very mild-mannered man off the field, Schmidt is transformed into a powerful defender during a game. His hair-trigger mind is quick to outguess the offense. He calls the defensive signals for the Lions; he plugs the middle and can engulf a quarterback with the ferocity of a jungle cat.

There were plenty of outstanding linebackers during the 1963 season. Helped by a good crop of front fours, men such as Bill George and Joe Fortunato of the Bears, Bill Forester of Green Bay, Pittsburgh's Myron Pottios, and the Rams' Jack Pardee were a sore spot for any team they played against. The Giants' games against Cleveland and Green Bay made Sam Huff the favorite of New York fans in recent years. To stop the likes of Jimmy Brown and Jimmy Taylor, the Giants' coaching staff set their defenses to have Huff key on these two, to move to any spot where Brown and Taylor were heading. The battles made for some rousing Sunday afternoons, and it was not unusual to hear the impact all the way up in the mezzanine broadcast booth. The Giants traded Huff this spring to the Washington Redskins, but that impact will never fade.

THE DEFENSIVE BACKS

The defensive backs form the rest of the support: two corner backs and two safety men. The corner backs are the closest to the line, and play to the outside of the corner linebackers. The safety men are the two farthest from the line of scrimmage and play to the inside of their corner backs. The defensive backs must be big enough to stop a running play and fast enough to cover the other team's best pass receiver, man to man. Since the corner backs are closer to the line of scrimmage than the safeties, they're generally bigger in size, as they occasionally blitz and are sometimes called upon to stop the running game.

Naturally the safety men will try for a tackle if they're the only thing standing between the runner and the goal line, but their primary responsibility is pass defense. The strong side safety man keys on the tight end, whether the end moves to the left or right. The weak side safety man keys on the split end, but can roam more freely and cover more territory because he has help from the weak-side corner back. The strong-side corner back is responsible for the flanker. This is the man-to-man type of pass defense and, of course, the backs and safety men get help from the linebackers, who will drop back for pass protection. In fact, the strong-side safety man can always rely on help from the strong-side linebacker, who will try to bump the tight end before he can head downfield. The strong-side linebacker is also responsible for protection against the flare or hook pass.

When watching defensive backs operate, notice how they keep the receivers either inside or outside, but never right on them, or, as the players say, never "head up on you." A three-yard distance is considered safe by most defensive backs, and they know if they allow a receiver to come head up on them, the receiver could get behind them, and that spells danger.

The Corner Backs

Of course, defensive backs realize a receiver will catch some passes during the course of a ball game. But they try to prevent the long touchdown pass, and they look for the stopper—the key interception.

Tom Brookshier, now a broadcasting colleague at WCAU in Philadelphia, was one of the league's all-time best corner backs. Tom, who played eight years for the Philadelphia Eagles, had his career abruptly ended on November 5, 1961, in a game with the Chicago Bears. While he was tackling Bears halfback Willie Galimore, Brookshier's right leg was shattered and he was forced to retire. The Eagles were 6–1 that day (their only loss to St. Louis by 3 points), and they managed to edge the Bears, 16–14, to boost their record to 7–1. But after Brookshier's departure the Eagles could do no better than a fifty-fifty split of the remaining six games, and the Eastern Conference crown went to the Giants.

Brookshier told me the two toughest men he ever had to cover on pass patterns were Cleveland's Ray Renfro, moving out of the flanker position, and Baltimore's Ray Berry. Neither dazzled him with a lot of speed, but their fakes were extraordinary. Brookshier credits much of Berry's success to quarterback Johnny Unitas, who is so quick to release the ball, the defender is usually out of position to cover.

In 1963 Dick Lynch of the Giants and Roosevelt Taylor of the Bears, both defensive halfbacks, led the league in pass interceptions with nine each. Lynch returned three of them for touchdowns, a new NFL record. The nine didn't come close to Dick "Night-Train" Lane's record fourteen, but it was nevertheless respectable.

The Safety Men

As far as safety men go, New York's Jimmy Patton is the finest in the game today. Jimmy's not big (5 foot 10, 180 pounds), but his cleverness makes up for his lack of size. Patton doubles up as a defensive coach and keeps a thorough book on every receiver in the NFL. He is himself an exceptional ball-hawk. In 1958 he led the league in interceptions, in 1961 he tied for second, and this past season he picked off six to tie for fourth.

As we mentioned earlier, safety men will cover either the tight or split end, depending on which side they are are playing on. But they will both key on the tight end to diagnose a possible running play. If the tight end throws a block on the defensive end or tackle, a run is usually on its way. (Corner backs, in addition to their pass-protection

assignments, will key on the offensive tackles or guards to get the tip-off on a running play.) When linemen pull out, it generally means they're forming interference for a run.

THE 4–3 DEFENSE

The 4–3 defense has many variations as far as assignments go. At times the front four slice to the inside, usually when they expect a running play in that direction or a straight power play. When this maneuver is used, the linebackers on the corners must check to the outside, and the middle linebacker must be alert to go either way. Then there's the 4–3 defense where the front four slice to the outside. Now, the linebackers must look to the inside. In a 4–3, too, the front four may shift to the strong or the weak side, with the linebackers, of course, compensating by moving to the unprotected side. These types of shifting maneuvers are naturally designed to throw off the offensive blocking and to rattle them enough to shake up their entire game plan. They often work. (See diagram on page 80.)

THE BLITZ

In obvious passing situations (third down and long yardage), the defense may use the weak-side safety blitz, in addition to red-dogging their linebackers. The weak-side safety man is used because he's the most expendable. He will wander all over the field in a man-to-man zone, unless the split end or flanker breaks into the middle. Then it's his job to cover.

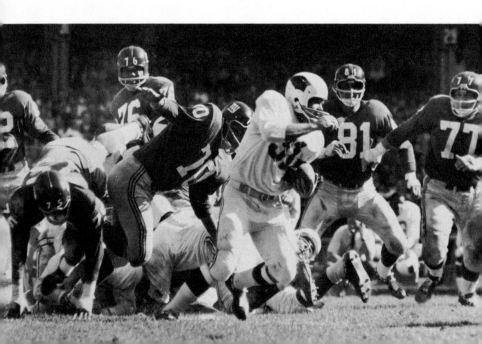

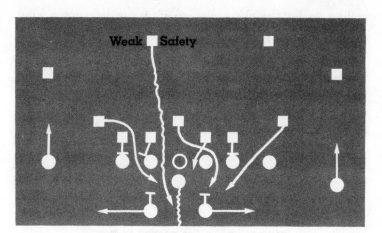

The Cardinals' weak-side safety blitz

The obvious aim of the blitz is to have as many men as possible rush the passer and keep him from throwing. In the St. Louis Cardinals' version of the weak-side safety blitz, which is similar to Detroit's, the corner linebackers rush from the outside toward the middle; the two defensive ends charge into the two offensive tackles, drawing their blocks. At the same time the two defensive tackles charge to their right, drawing the blocks of the offensive guards. The middle linebacker slashes left and red-dogs between the tackle and the guard, and the weak-side safety, who has cheated a step or two forward prior to the snap, flies between the center and the offensive left guard (see diagram).

If a team does employ the weak-side safety blitz, you'll notice the remaining safety and both corner backs covering the two ends and the flanker back, man for man.

There are naturally risks when the safety blitz is used. The big danger is that the halfback or the fullback will slide outside for the short pass, but the defense is often willing to let the short one go if it can prevent a long yardage completion. Another obvious danger is tipping off the offense. An alert quarterback, figuring the blitz is on, will call the draw play or the quick pass to his tight end right over the middle. In this case, he will simply take the pass from center, generally on a quick count (a low number such as one), stand straight up, and pop.

THE 6-1 DEFENSE

Another defense frequently seen in the NFL is the 6-1, which offensive teams sometimes mistake for the 4-3, because the linebackers don't actually move that much from their 4-3 positions. The 6-1 is used for red-dogging, but it is also effective against a team which

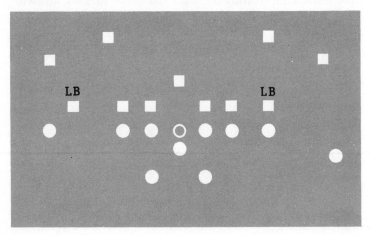

The 6-1 defense

does a lot of running. It's often used inside the ten, when the goal-line stand is in its beginning, or five-to-ten-yard, stage. Down closer to the goal line, the 8–3 is used, with all the big boys up front. In the 6–1, the corner line-backers move up toward the line of scrimmage and, de-pending upon the down and position on the field, will either blitz to the inside or position for the run (see diagram).

BLOCKING THE FIELD GOAL

In defending against the field goal, strategies are worked out the week before to take advantage of the opposing team's weaknesses. The rush generally comes from the outside and is put on by the corner linebackers and the corner backs, with perhaps the weak-side safety also joining the blitz. The defensive ends and tackles may try to open holes up front to let the middle line-backer crash through as well. The defenders make a strong effort to put themselves between the kicked ball and the goal posts before the ball has a chance to rise. The place-kicker is only seven yards behind his center, the same distance the quarterback travels before throwing a pass. Of course, the quarterback usually gets at least three seconds to throw the ball. The kicker meets the ball with his toe within a second after it leaves the center's hands. But if the defender moves for the line of trajectory, he's apt to block the kick even as far away as the line of scrimmage.

BLOCKING THE PUNT

It's much more difficult to block a punt, for the simple reasons that the kicker is a good fourteen yards behind the line of scrimmage, and his line of trajectory is more severe than the place kicker's. Usually, when the offense is in punt formation, the defensive linemen charge in just far enough to make the punter commit himself. When they're sure it's a legitimate punt, they peel off to set up a blocking wall for the receiver. A defensive unit that takes a punt for granted and immediately moves back to block without crossing the line of scrimmage is asking

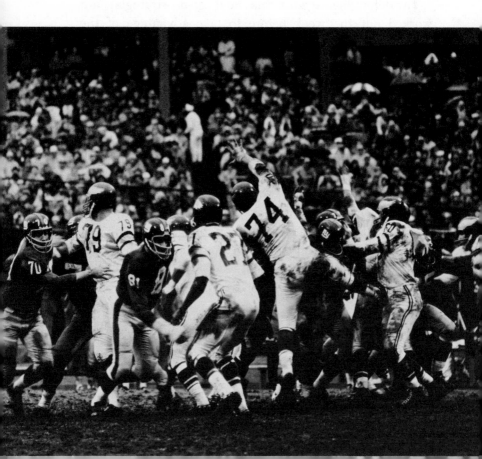

for trouble. This happened against the San Francisco Forty-Niners on October 6, 1963. Detroit's Yale Lary, the league's leading punter, noticed early in the game that the Forty-Niners weren't rushing on punt formation. He faked his next attempt and ran the ball for a 27-yard gain. The entire San Francisco defense was weak that afternoon. The Lions won the game, 26-3.

Remember, in field-goal and punt formations, there's always the chance of the fake, so the defenses must adjust accordingly. In the case of the extra point, there's usually no fake involved. The extra-point kickers in the NFL are so skilled, they seldom miss. So the defensive unit will try to send all eleven men in to attempt a block. Some teams will even pyramid their men, in an effort to prevent the point. But the snap from center and the ensuing kick happen so quickly, you'll rarely see one blocked.

CONCLUSION

Defensive ball players don't often experience the joys of scoring touchdowns. So they have to get their kicks elsewhere. Their kicks are in hard-nose football; the rougher, the better. Defensive ball players are a proud lot, with tremendous desire. On the Tuesday afternoon before the Giants' final game of the 1963 season, I asked Tom Scott, the veteran linebacker of eleven years, how much longer he thought he could play. He answered without hesitation. "It's still no problem for me to get in shape. My legs still feel good, and my speed hasn't left me. And," he added, "the desire is still here." His thumb firmly thumped a spot in the vicinity of his heart.

4. TV Has Sound, Too!

Perhaps I'm blowing my own horn, but, speaking for all my colleagues who earn their living by reporting what they see, let me remind you that your television sets are equipped with audio as well as video.

In doing the play-by-play telecasts of the Giants' games, both home and away, I work with Pat Summerall, the former kicking great, who closed out his pro career with New York. Both Pat and I have access to much information about the team. First of all, the coaching staff is well aware of the fact that we can be trusted not to divulge any game plans. Second, we have made it our business to take a sincere interest in the players and their lives, off the field as well as on. So we have their confidence. This closeness to the coaches and players gives us a vast amount of knowledge which we attempt to pass along to our viewers and "listeners."

Every Tuesday at noon during the football season, the Mara Brothers, the owners of the Giants, are hosts at a luncheon in the private clubroom located on the mezzanine level of Yankee Stadium. In attendance are the Giants' coaching staff, the public-relations director of New York's next opponent, and members of the press, radio, and television. Following the meal, the coaches sum up the previous Sunday's game and preview the upcoming clash. The team physician runs down the injury list, giving his diagnosis and prognosis for each player. Then the visiting P.R. man expounds on *his* team. Much of this meeting can be very helpful to the broadcaster.

But the most important part of the Tuesday meeting comes next. Everyone is invited to visit the Giants' dressing room and meet the players individually. Now you find out that the doctor is taking 100 cc's of fluid from Jack Stroud's knee every third day, but Stroud says he'll be ready Sunday. If Stroud's leg buckles during the game, you know why and inform the audience of the true facts. Frank Gifford reports that his back still hurts from last Sunday's game, and if it doesn't ease up in the next day or two he'll be benching it on Sunday. The coaches are studying a game film in the back office, and you walk in and learn about a certain pass pattern or a defensive maneuver. Alex Webster is under the heat lamp, and he confides he's worried about his future career, the lower back hurts that badly. You walk out of the locker room an hour later with a notebook full of material, and it becomes an important part of your game plan for Sunday.

That notebook of mine, which gets to every ball game, also contains the names and numbers of all the players on both clubs for the coming week. There's also a section of offensive statistics, a complete list of each player's record for the current year and past years. There's another similar section for the defensive players. I also outline all the possibilities of how a win or a loss will affect the standings.

During the game itself I keep a complete running account of everything that happens, so I can accurately recap the game in the wrap-up. This summary also serves as reference material throughout the course of the game.

About nine o'clock on the morning of a game, the Giants have breakfast. In New York the Roosevelt Hotel is breakfast headquarters. On the road it's wherever the Giants are staying. The menus are preplanned, although there is a choice, from juice and oatmeal to steak and eggs. *No one* attends these breakfasts except the team members, the owners, the coaches, Pat Summerall, and me!

Again, Pat and I are there because the entire Giants' organization knows we can be trusted. When breakfast is over, a game-plan meeting is held in the same room. It's a blackboard refresher, with the head coach and his assistants detailing every aspect of the offensive and defensive game plan. All the "secrets" are laid out before me in this thirty-minute skull session. When I'm up in that broadcast booth, there are no surprises. I know exactly what's going on.

At times, though, judging from some of the mail I receive, viewers get the impression I have no idea about the game, let alone the game plan. There's a good reason for not revealing game plans ahead of the opening kick-off, or predicting what may come up on ensuing plays. In a game in 1962, the Giants discovered that a member of the staff of the opposing team had been planted in the TV mobile unit to monitor our telecast and was relaying the information back to their bench. New York barely won that ball game, and we were asked by the Giants' front office to limit our "forecasting." We have kept their respect by doing just that.

After the post-breakfast meeting, the team leaves for the stadium by bus. I make a last visit to the dressing room about noontime and again visit as many players as possible before the room is cleared of all visitors. My final question before leaving is usually addressed to head coach Allie Sherman. "Any dipsy-doodles, Allie?" Sherman will smile and obligingly detail one last play—the "dipsy-doodle."

The broadcasting booth is a complex of men, microphones, cables, and electronic equipment, including the monitor, which is like any home television set. My attention is divided between the field and the monitor, with the monitor getting about 70 per cent of my viewing. In this way, I see what you see, and describe only what you see. The other details outside of camera range can be filled in between downs. The monitor can be most important in those stadiums where the booth is in an unfavorable position, since it aids in accurate reporting.

Because you at home can see what's happening, I strive not to talk too much. Constant chatter, I think, can be annoying to the viewer. Let the picture tell the story, with the announcer simply serving to supplement the action whenever necessary. My color man can add his expert commentary derived from having played the game, and this combination, coupled with the picture, keeps the viewer as well informed as he can be.

A further aid to me in the booth is my statistician, who keeps me continually informed on first downs, length of runbacks, rushing and passing yardage, and all the other vital information which I can pass on to you.

Last, but not least, are my spotter, Bill Friel, and my magnetic spotting board. Friel has been with me a long time and knows exactly how I work. He knows football thoroughly, has a keen mind and quick reflexes. He's a hell of a right hand. The spotting board itself is 16 by 26 inches, with one side colored blue and white, the colors of the Giants, and the other side colored with the hues of the opposing team. Little magnetic blocks, representing each player on both teams, are numbered to correspond to the players' uniforms. These blocks are placed on the board just as the players are on the field. Say the Giants have the ball, and Phil King has carried. My spotter picks out King's block with his name and number on it, the block, of course, colored in blue and white. The spotter also picks the block or blocks corresponding to the player or players making the tackle. To prevent the microphone from picking up unpleasant scraping sounds of metal rubbing on metal, we have had the board covered with a green felt material similar to the covering on pool tables.

You now pretty much have the entire inside story. All you need is the picture in proper focus; lots of cheese dip, potato chips, and your favorite beverage close at hand, and your next-door neighbor in the chair beside yours. You might even permit the presence of your wife and kids, since they now know all about the game from reading this book. Next you turn and say, "A definite pass play coming up—so watch for the blitz!"

APPENDIX I

The Officials

There are five officials assigned to every professional football game: the referee, the umpire, the head linesman, the field judge, and the back judge. Each is assigned to specific areas of the field, and each has definite responsibilities. They all enforce the official rules. The referee has the added job of flipping the coin before the start of the game to determine which team will kick off and which team will defend which goal. The umpire is given the added responsibility of keeping the official time.

The National Football League has assembled the finest group of officials I have ever had the pleasure of meeting. They are a dedicated group of men, highly respected on the football field as well as in their other fields of endeavor. They have gained the confidence of the players, which makes it easier to maintain discipline during the ball game.

You may notice what looks to be a sixth official on the

field, usually wearing a white cap or a red glove. He's not a paid official of the National Football League, but a salaried employee of the television network. He's the fellow who's responsible for getting in eighteen "breaks" for TV commercials. If, for example, there are no scores or time-outs in the first five minutes of the game, he will signal the referee, who will call for a time-out. If this is annoying to you, please try to remember who picks up the freight for these telecasts. · Without the sponsors, it might be almost impossible to bring the games into your home.

During the course of the game the officials' red hand-kerchiefs will fly from time to time, indicating an infraction of the rules which calls for a penalty. A guide to the officials' penalty signals and general signals will be found on the endpapers.

Glossary

Automatics: Signals by which quarterback changes play call at line of scrimmage; also known as audibles, or check signals.

Balance: A player, usually a back, so sure on his feet he is difficult to topple.

Balanced Line: Three linemen, guard, tackle, and end, on either side of the center.

Basic "T" Offense: Tight balanced line and backfield.

Blitz: Crashing defensive back, usually weak-side safety, aiming to stop quarterback.

Bomb: Long, high forward pass to deep receiver.

Bootleg: Deceptive play where quarterback heads in opposite direction to offensive flow, concealing ball along his thigh.

Bread-and-Butter Play: A sure yardage gainer for offense.

Cutback: When a ball player, heading to the outside, suddenly changes direction sharply to the inside.

Dive Play: A short gainer through the middle of the line.

Double-Teaming: Two offensive linemen blocking one defender; two defenders guarding one receiver.

Double Wing: An offensive formation where both halfbacks line up just behind or to the outside of their ends, almost creating a double-flanker situation. Quarterback may, or may not line up directly behind his center, as in the "T" or the shotgun formation.

Down and Out: Pass receiver runs straight downfield and then cuts to the outside.

Eat the Ball: Passer is tackled before he has a chance to throw the ball.

Fair Catch: While a kick, which has traveled past the line of scrimmage, is in flight, the receiver raises one arm at full length to signal he will not attempt a runback. Ball must be caught to be ruled dead.

Flanker: Halfback who lines up wide of his end.

Flare Pass: Pass thrown to backfield man who has run wide behind his line of scrimmage.

Flood Area: All eligible pass receivers head for a designated zone on the field.

Flow of Play: Direction in which play is headed.

Getting "Up": Conditioning oneself emotionally for upcoming game.

Hash-Marks: In-bounds lines on playing field, 20 yards from sidelines, where ball is put in play at minimum distance from sideline.

Hook Pattern: Pass receiver, usually the end, moves upfield to a designated point and suddenly turns to face his quarterback; this play is sometimes called a turn-in pass.

"I" Formation: Four backs line up directly behind the center.

Keying: A defender guiding himself by the moves of one or more offensive players.

Long Man: Deepest receiver in pass patterns.

Look-in Pass: Quarterback straightens up immediately after ball is snapped and fires short pass, usually to tight end; sometimes called quick pop.

Man-for-Man: Pass defense where one defensive man protects against one receiver.

Mousetrap: An offensive guard pulls out of line to block defensive tackle or end who has been "permitted" to crash in.

Option Play: Ball carrier can either run or pass.

Pitchout: Quarterback takes pass from center, wheels, and immediately releases an underhand toss to one of his backs, who is usually in motion.

Plays Loose: As defensive back, doesn't get too close to fast pass receivers.

Pocket: An area 7 yards directly behind the offensive center to which the quarterback fades for maximum protection on a pass play.

Pursuit: Defense continues to follow play until whistle blows play dead.

Quarterback Sneak: Quarterback takes snap from center and plunges straight ahead.

Quick Opener: Short plunge through line with no faking involved prior to initial handoff.

Red-Dog: Crashing linebacker going for quarterback immediately after ball is snapped; sometimes applied to other defensive backs (*see* Blitz).

Reverse: Ball carrier goes opposite to flow of play.

Sagging Middle: Weak center of line.

Screen Pass: Starts out like basic pass pattern, with most receivers heading upfield and passer retreating 7 yards to pocket; center, guard, and tackle brush block on line and then release laterally to the outside to form a screen which hides the receiver. If pass is completed, three linemen form blocking pattern.

Secondary: Defensive backfield.

Second Effort: Player's attempt, after carrying out initial assignment, to be helpful elsewhere.

Shotgun Offense: Quarterback positioned behind the center a predetermined distance away; other backs and ends are spread wide and close to line of scrimmage.

Single Wing: Line is unbalanced; pass from center is to a back through center's legs; four backs, tailback, fullback, blocking back, and wingback. Tailback lines up on weak side about five yards behind or slightly to the inside of the guard; fullback is four yards behind the center or slightly to his outside; the blocking back is between the strong-side guard and tackle, and about a yard and a half behind the line; and the wingback is outside the strong-side end, similar to the flanker in the "T," although not spread.

Slotback: Halfback who lines up directly behind the hole created by the end splitting and is used for pitchouts and as a pass receiver.

Split or Spread End: End lined up very wide of tackle, usually at least 6 or 7 yards away.

Taxi Squad: Players who are under contract to a team, engage in its practice sessions, but are not included in the official roster. Can be activated at any time to complete roster depleted by injury or trade.

Tertiary: Began being used to describe defensive corner backs and safety men when linebackers began dropping back more frequently for additional pass protection.

Tight End: End lined up close to his tackle; used a great deal on blocking assignments in addition to pass-receiving duties.

Three-Point Stance: Crouch, with one hand resting on the ground.

Two on One: Two offensive players block one defensive man (*see* Double-Teaming).

Zone Defense: A pass defense where each defensive man is responsible for a designated area of playing field.

Officials' Signals

1

OFFSIDE, ENCROACHING, or FREE KICK VIOLATION

Hands on hips.

Encroaching—same signal followed by placement of hand on head.

2

CRAWLING, PUSHING, or HELPING RUNNER

Pushing movement of hands to front with arms downward.

3

ILLEGAL MOTION AT SNAP

Horizontal arc with either hand.

4

ILLEGAL FORWARD PASS

Waving hands behind back.

INTENTIONAL GROUNDING OF PASS

Same as above followed by raised hand flung downward.

5

PERSONAL FOUL

Striking of one wrist above head.

Roughing Kicker—same signal followed by swinging leg.

Running into Passer—same signal followed by raised arm swung forward.

Clipping—same signal followed by striking back of calf with hand.

Unnecessary Roughness—

Piling—

Grabbing Face Mask—

6

INTERFERENCE WITH FAIR CATCH or FORWARD PASS

Pushing hands forward from shoulder with hand vertical.

INELIGIBLE MAN DOWNFIELD

Chopping motion of hands with arms extended.

7

HOLDING or ILLEGAL USE of HANDS or ARMS

Grasping of one wrist at chest level.

8

DELAY OF GAME or EXCESS TIME-OUT

Folded arms.

9

TOUCHDOWN, FIELD GOAL, or SUCCESSFUL TRY

Both arms extended above head.